ANTIRACIST BY DESIGN

ANTIRACIST BY DESIGN

Reimagining Applied Behavioral Science

CRYSTAL C. HALL AND MINDY HERNANDEZ

The MIT Press
Cambridge, Massachusetts
London, England

© 2024 Crystal C. Hall and Mindy Hernandez

All rights reserved. No part of this book may be used to train artificial intelligence systems or reproduced in any form by any electronic or mechanical means (including photocopying, recording, or information storage and retrieval) without permission in writing from the publisher.

The MIT Press would like to thank the anonymous peer reviewers who provided comments on drafts of this book. The generous work of academic experts is essential for establishing the authority and quality of our publications. We acknowledge with gratitude the contributions of these otherwise uncredited readers.

This book was set in Adobe Garamond and Berthold Akzidenz Grotesk by Jen Jackowitz. Printed and bound in the United States of America.

Library of Congress Cataloging-in-Publication Data

Names: Hall, Crystal Celestine, 1981– author. | Hernandez, Mindy, author.
Title: Antiracist by design : reimagining applied behavioral science / Crystal C. Hall and Mindy Hernandez.
Description: Cambridge, Massachusetts : The MIT Press, [2024] | Includes bibliographical references and index.
Identifiers: LCCN 2024004619 (print) | LCCN 2024004620 (ebook) | ISBN 9780262549462 (paperback) | ISBN 9780262380423 (epub) | ISBN 9780262380430 (pdf)
Subjects: LCSH: Racism in the social sciences. | Racism in psychology. | Anti-racism.
Classification: LCC H61.35 .H35 2024 (print) | LCC H61.35 (ebook) | DDC 300.8—dc23/eng/20240307
LC record available at https://lccn.loc.gov/2024004619
LC ebook record available at https://lccn.loc.gov/2024004620

10 9 8 7 6 5 4 3 2 1

For Noah, Carter, and Simone

For Lula and Oliver. But most of all, to Victor Luis Hernandez and Delia Visbal Hernandez

Contents

Preface *ix*
Definitions *xiii*

INTRODUCTION *1*

I THE PROMISE AND FUNDAMENTAL FLAW OF APPLIED BEHAVIORAL SCIENCE

1 **APPLIED BEHAVIORAL SCIENCE: KEY INSIGHTS AND CRITICAL OVERSIGHTS** *19*

2 **WHAT'S AT STAKE AND WHAT'S POSSIBLE** *33*

3 **WHY WE LOOK AWAY, AND WHAT'S POSSIBLE WHEN WE DON'T** *45*

4 **BEHAVIORAL SCIENCE IN ACTION: STANDARD TOOLS AND PRACTICES** *55*

5 **A VISION OF SUCCESS** *69*

II THE ROADMAP TO CHANGE

6 **PREPARE YOUR WORKPLACE** *77*

7 **PARTNER AND CODEFINE** *85*

8 **CODISCOVER** *91*

9 **CODESIGN** *97*

10 IMPLEMENT AND INTERPRET *105*

11 SHARE, ADAPT, AND SCALE *117*

12 ACTION AGENDA *125*

13 CONCLUSION *135*

Acknowledgments *139*
Appendix: Resources *145*
Notes *153*
Index *171*

Preface

> The truth is, I've never cared for the National
> Anthem. If you think about it, it's not a good
> song. Too high for most of us with "the rockets
> red glare" and then there are the bombs.
> . . .
> And what of the stanzas
> we never sing, the third that mentions "no refuge
> could save the hireling and the slave"? Perhaps,
> the truth is, every song of this country
> has an unsung third stanza, something brutal
> snaking underneath us as we blindly sing
> the high notes with a beer sloshing in the stands
> hoping our team wins. . . .
> —EXCERPTED FROM "A NEW NATIONAL ANTHEM," BY ADA LIMÓN

This book has been a long time in the making.

On the surface, we were inspired to write this book in the wake of the worldwide 2020 protests calling for a reckoning due to the murder of George Floyd and many other Black Americans. In the spring of 2021, we published a commentary piece for the *Behavioral Scientist* in which we urged behavioral science scholars and practitioners to join the work necessary to dismantle the racist and white-centered approaches we have always taken in our work.[1] As we researched that piece, it became painfully obvious that this perspective is largely missing from our field. As behavioral science researchers and practitioners who care deeply about our work, we have more to say, and this book allows us to explore these ideas in depth.

When we started writing this book, we watched the COVID-19 pandemic unfold with vastly different consequences for people of color. Black, Indigenous, People of Color (BIPOC) were one and a half times more likely to be infected with COVID-19, twice as likely to be hospitalized and as of 2022, twice as likely to die of their infection, compared to their white counterparts.[2]

Now, more than four years later, most Americans have put the pandemic behind them, but researchers are discovering COVID's residual fingerprints on BIPOC communities. In 2023, the U.S. Census Bureau found that Latino and Black households are more likely than any other group to struggle with long COVID.[3] BIPOC children are disproportionately grieving lost parents—a staggering 65 percent of children who lost a primary caregiver to COVID are from BIPOC communities.[4] The pandemic is over and our interest has waned, but the underlying issues that contributed to these devastating effects remain.

For example, the climate crisis continues to be an existential threat, but its greatest harms affect the most vulnerable. In the United States, Black and Latino communities are exposed to a greater amount of air pollution than they produce, and research indicates that the poorest counties in the country will be the most financially impacted by the climate crisis.[5] Unsurprisingly, people of color disproportionately call these counties home. In the summer of 2020, as we initiated our collaboration on this topic, we could literally see this crisis unfolding from our respective windows. The wildfire smoke suffocating Seattle, where Crystal lives, dimmed the sun in Washington, DC, where Mindy lives. These events served as a catalyst for writing this book and a reminder of the challenges we face, but the issues we explore in this book are far from novel.

Really, our path to writing this book began long before we penned that commentary at the height of racial unrest (in our lifetimes) in the United States. As two women of color with decades of experience in this field, we have witnessed the daily challenges of working in an environment that centers the wealthy, white, male perspective. We have been told that "We don't have to go into all of this race stuff" by the leader of a large, influential organization. We have been ordered to change comments for a public event by a foundation leader who plainly stated that "we don't say race and class at this foundation." We have felt personally hurt by a colleague who, during a conversation about racism weeks after the murder of George Floyd, openly attempted to change the topic. Others stood by when this happened, silent. While leading important work on diversity and inclusion, we have been plainly asked "what is the point?" In other conversations, it has been suggested that work being done to understand the racial and ethnic breakdown of scholars within the field was simply to show that we were "trying hard on diversity issues." When asking a colleague why he didn't disaggregate data to examine impacts on Black participants, he simply replied "[understanding different impacts for Black participants] was not our goal."

In conversations that *did* shift to race, we have heard awkward language about "crayon colors" from our academic colleagues, government collaborators, and powerful private-sector leaders who tried to avoid talking directly about race and, more importantly, racism. We have been in countless meetings at very high levels in which interventions aimed at poverty, education, and health in America are discussed without the words race or racism ever being uttered. These experiences are not new or unique to us, but they continue to provide evidence of a problematic pattern in our field.

At best, we have occasionally spoken up (but more often remained silent in the face of pushback). At worst, we have reinforced the problem by failing to openly address the racist structures that underlie many of the problems we've attempted to tackle in our work. This book intends to map a better way forward, both for people like us who are regularly confronted with situations like these and for anyone who wants to move human behavior toward equity and justice.

Until we can directly and openly address our racist research practices, the reach of their findings will be limited. More dangerously, we risk inadvertently strengthening racist structures, practices, and policies. As a field, we have collectively chosen to design around systemic racism as if it doesn't exist. The goal of this book is to break this silence and begin the hard work of directly naming, addressing, and attempting to resolve these problems.

An antiracist approach to applied behavioral science will be challenging, but we believe it's possible—and imperative.

This is the first book to identify the challenge of creating antiracist behavioral design and to provide tools and a roadmap to implementation. It's for all who seek to design programs, policies, or products that aim to make the world a better, more just place. We each have a role to play in the fight toward racial justice. When we fail to play our role, we become part of the problem. But the opposite is also true: by leaning into our ambition and optimism to design for the world we want, rather than the one we have, we move the field and fight for justice forward. This book maps out the first steps for scholars, practitioners, and all of those interested in applied behavioral science and design.

Along the way, it's also our goal to uplift and amplify the work of other scholars and thought leaders whose voices and perspectives directly relate to ours. We know that we haven't been alone in considering these important issues, and we humbly recognize the work that has deeply inspired, enlightened, and motivated us. We acknowledge that meaningful steps have been taken toward incorporating antiracist approaches in other disciplines, efforts from which there's much to learn.

We're grateful that you've chosen to take this journey with us. The ride ahead won't be smooth, and it will never be finished. But that doesn't mean we shouldn't get started. The impacts of racism are deep and pervasive, so we truly can't afford to waste time. As the reader, we hope that this book will help you to recognize where you (like us) may have missed opportunities to tackle racism head on. More importantly, we offer suggestions for how behavioral science fans and advocates (scholars and practitioners alike) can improve the way we wield these deeply important tools and be part of a better way forward. Let's get started.

Definitions

La lengua es la ametralladora de la libertad.

—TATO LAVIERA

Throughout this book, we'll use terms specific to the fields of social and behavioral science and the work of social justice scholars and activists. Concise definitions of these terms appear below.

Antiracist: One who, through their actions or expressions, supports efforts that produce or sustain racial equity between racial groups.

Applied behavioral science: Multidisciplinary field of study that draws on insights from the social sciences (including psychology and behavioral economics) to develop effective interventions to promote positive behavior and improve outcomes in various settings, such as health care, public policy, and the workplace. It aims to address problems occurring outside of the lab, in the real world.

Bias: Unfair evaluation of an individual based on that person's membership in a particular group or category, such as a racial or ethnic group or gender, rather than on individual merit.

Explicit bias refers to the attitudes and beliefs we have about a person or group, operating on a conscious level.

Implicit bias refers to the brain's automatic, instant association of stereotypes or attitudes toward particular groups. These biases can be deeply ingrained and can lead to discriminatory behaviors, even if someone consciously believes in equality.

Behavioral economics: Field of study that examines how psychological, cognitive, and emotional factors have an impact on decision-making and behavior, often focused on how they differ from those predicted by classical economic theories.

Behavioral science: Field encompassing a range of disciplines that study human behavior, including psychology, sociology, anthropology, economics, and political science. It involves the scientific study of human actions, interactions, and motivations to better understand and predict behavior.

BIPOC/People of color: A person-first acronym that refers to Black, Indigenous, and people of color. It is a term used to describe individuals from diverse racial and ethnic backgrounds who share experiences and histories of struggles against racism and colonization.

Class: Refers to the economic status of a group of individuals, based on factors such as income, wealth, and education.

Classical economic theory: Field of study that presumes that economies and markets operate based on self-regulated forces that follow the natural flow of production and exchange. In these theories, individual actors are presumed to act rationally and in their own best interest.

Culture: The ways of living, including values, beliefs, aesthetic standards, linguistic expression, patterns of thinking, behavioral norms, and styles of communication that a group of people has developed.

Diversity: Representation of a range of individual, social, and demographic characteristics within a group or population.

Discrimination: Behavior directed toward an individual that is based upon their identity (such as race or gender) rather than their individual merit.

Ethnicity: A social categorization referring to the sharing of a common culture, including shared origin; shared psychological characteristics and attitudes; and shared language, religion, and cultural traditions.

Equality: The state or process of treating everyone the same.

Equity: The state or process of being fair and just.

Identity: The many ways in which individuals define themselves.

Inclusion: A state or process of being a part of a group or society that values the inherent worth and contribution of all group members, along with providing the group members with dignity and respect.

Intersectionality: A concept rooted in Black feminism, and more recently used in reference to a term coined by the legal scholar Kimberlé Crenshaw to describe how multiple forms of inequality can operate together and exacerbate each other.

Nudge: Any aspect of the choice architecture that alters people's behavior in a predictable way without (1) forbidding any options or (2) significantly changing their economic incentives. To count as a nudge, the intervention must (3) be easy and cheap to avoid and (4) significantly alter the behavior of "humans" even though it would be ignored by "Econs."[1]

Oppression: Systematic mistreatment of people based upon their membership in a group, including the denial of full access to power and resources.

Positionality: The social and political forces that create a person's individual identity and their outlook and biases in the world.

Prejudice: Negative opinions and beliefs about a social group that are formed without sufficient evidence.

Privilege: Access to benefits, power, and resources (economic, social, political) that others do not have, based on one's group membership.

Public policy: The set of rules and actions taken by a government, at any level, to govern a society and address real-world challenges.

Race: A group perceived to share some physical characteristics. While these categories are socially and politically constructed and do not have a biological basis, they have significant social and cultural meaning in many societies.

Racism: The systematic oppression of a group of people based on their membership in a racial group that the dominant group deems inferior.

Structural racism: The ways that a society perpetuates racial discrimination by reinforcing unjust social and political systems such as housing, education, and employment. This book takes liberties with this term and uses it synonymously with *institutional racism*, though there are subtle differences between the two.

Individual racism: Personal beliefs toward other races that impact the way an individual treats individuals from a particular race or racial group.

Racist:[2] One who is supporting measures that produce or sustain racial inequity between racial groups through their actions or inaction or by expressing racist ideas.

Racist policy: Any measure that produces or sustains racial inequity between racial groups.

Social justice: Active engagement acting toward diversity, equity, and inclusion.

Stereotype: A simplified conception of an individual based on their identity or group membership.

White fragility: A state in which even a minimum amount of racial stress becomes intolerable for white people, triggering a range of defensive moves. These behaviors function to reinstate white racial supremacy.

White supremacy/White superiority: A system or social order that keeps power and resources consolidated among white elites, using an ideology that upholds whiteness—including white people, white cultural values, and white institutions—as being best and most "normal."

INTRODUCTION

> I'm no longer accepting the things I cannot change . . . I'm changing the things I cannot accept.
>
> —ANGELA DAVIS

In 2010, just as behavioral science—the study of how and why people behave in the wacky, wild, and sometimes wondrous ways we do—was leaping into the world of public policy, we found ourselves sitting on cold metal chairs in a free tax preparation center in Philadelphia.

We watched people stream in the door, bracing against freezing rain, eager to get help filing their taxes. Pinching and expanding that moment into a close-up, our role was straightforward. We were there to help ("nudge") the people in the waiting room—all tax filers with low incomes—save some of their tax returns. The assumption was that even small amounts of savings could buffer against financial shocks, paving a way to economic security and even mobility. When we zoom out of this moment, we can see we were part of something bigger. We were among the early experimenters testing the enticing but embryonic promise of applying behavioral insights to America's social challenges. The potential matched the risks of getting it wrong.

It was an exciting time for those of us who studied human behavior. Academic researchers were diving into ambitious collaborations with governments and nonprofits, philanthropists were inviting behavioral scientists to discuss how our field could respond to global dilemmas like poverty and child mortality, and in short order, world leaders like President Barack Obama and Prime Minister David Cameron were investing in applied behavioral science at the highest levels of government as a promising way to design a better world.

As young professionals, we arrived in Philly and in this fascinating field just as behavioral science was poised to make its big break. We both had the opportunity to study with the late Daniel Kahneman, honored as one of the founders of modern behavioral science, at Princeton University shortly after he received the 2002 Nobel Prize in Economic Sciences. He received the award for his groundbreaking research incorporating psychological insights into economic science with his longtime friend and collaborator Amos Tversky. About a decade later, we were two of the first team members on the US version of the United Kingdom's Behavioural Insights Team (BIT)—the Social and Behavioral Scienced Team (SBST)—established during the Obama administration.[1] The opportunity to bring this work to the US federal government was so exciting that Crystal paused her teaching and research as a tenure-track professor to move to Washington, DC, for a year and Mindy flew from Mozambique, where she was living at the time, just to be part of the first full team meeting.

Back in Philly, we were thrilled to be part of what felt like a groundbreaking attempt to capture insights from social theories to improve people's lives. But as we sat together, looking around and jotting down notes, we felt a growing unease. It wasn't random that most of the folks in the waiting room were BIPOC and looked more like our families than our fellow behavioral scientists. (Neither of us had ever had a Black or Latino[2] behavioral science professor, which was unsurprising given that data indicates that in 2013, Black and Latino researchers accounted for under 4 percent of the workforce in behavioral and social sciences research).[3]

In America, debt and wealth aren't race neutral.[4] Black and Latino families are far less likely to have access to employer-sponsored retirement accounts and more likely to be denied loans regardless of credit score.[5] In addition, Black workers earn 76 cents, Latino workers earn 73 cents, and Indigenous workers earn 77 cents for every dollar earned by white workers.[6] These disparities reflect historic discrimination and ongoing structural racism, not individual choices like the one-time savings decision at a tax site that we were there to influence.

Our emerging field was about shifting choices. But in America, skin color often narrows the choices available. Still, our job wasn't to notice that or to name the racist policies and practices that lead to it, and our job certainly wasn't to use behavioral insights to respond to it.

We designed and ran a few simple interventions in tax sites in Philly that focused on individual-level biases, designed to respond to systemic "errors in judgment" instead of responding to—or even acknowledging—systemic errors like racism and inequity. Perhaps unsurprisingly, our interventions had little effect.

Over the years, this situation repeated itself in different forms and our discomfort grew. Together, we bring almost forty years of experience engaging in behavioral research in academic settings, in nonprofits, and with governments at all levels—in the United States and abroad. As a result, we've seen the field's shortcomings up close.

For example, we worked to encourage people on federal assistance to join work training and educational advancement opportunities, leaning into America's story that economic returns to education can overcome structural barriers like race-based economic exclusion. We never acknowledged that the financial returns on education are different for BIPOC.

But Chris Rock did when he described his neighbors: "[My only three black neighbors are] Mary J. Blige, one of the greatest singers of all time, Denzel Washington, one of the greatest actors of all time, and Jay-Z, one of the greatest rappers of all time." His white neighbor? "A dentist. And he isn't like the greatest dentist in history either. I had to host the Oscars to get that house—a black dentist in my neighborhood would have to invent teeth."[7]

Chris Rock has a point. Black people attain more years of schooling and credentials than white people from families with comparable resources but have less to show for it: Black households headed by a college graduate have, on average, *less* wealth than those headed by white *high school dropouts*. Returns to employment are different too. White families where the head of the household is unemployed have double the wealth of a Black family where the head of the household is employed full time.[8]

We also worked on projects to improve the health behaviors of people living in poverty, but our interventions never took into account that BIPOC are less likely to have access to health care and more likely to be exposed to lead-contaminated water, pollution, and toxic waste. Additionally, Black mothers and their babies—regardless of income—are about twice as likely to die as white mothers and their babies during childbirth.

We plugged along, ignoring our nagging intuition that our designs and interventions were failing to account for something enormous and that this oversight might be blunting the promise of our work, or worse, creating unintended consequences that hurt the very people we were trying to help.

Meanwhile, the field of behavioral science grew to touch human decision-making in almost every domain—from COVID-19 vaccine campaigns to college financial aid forms. More than five hundred behavioral science units now sit in the biggest companies in the world (Walmart, Pepsi, IKEA) and in some of the largest and most powerful countries on the planet. Today, social scientists have a seat at the policy table and an entry point into the lives of millions, which is why it's so urgent to correct our glaring oversights.

Throughout the field's rise, we have failed to name and challenge the racial injustices fundamental to many of the issues we work on. Instead, we put a postracial frame around our work and focus on social mobility broadly, ignoring race-specific barriers as if structural racism were an unfortunate mess for someone else to clean up.

As popularly understood, the term structural racism can seem vague and notional. But it points to specific policies and practices that embed ancient brutality, past injustice, and present prejudices into every aspect of American life, from our legal and educational systems to our housing and lending practices. These policies systematically excluded people of color from opportunities and benefits, and that exclusion has created long, sticky tails of inequity that manifest in the yawning gaps between white and BIPOC populations in wealth, health, education, employment, and housing that persist today.

Applied behavioral science has launched interventions focused on each of these areas, often considering poverty and classism while avoiding race and racism. As a result, we created nudges aimed at the tail-end manifestations of structural racism while never mentioning the original exclusion. Perhaps this was because to gain traction in the early days, the field wanted to define itself in wide, nonpartisan strokes and reach as large an audience as possible. Maybe tackling individual-level barriers seemed more feasible. Or possibly the field just fell under the gravitational pull of powerful interests vested in upholding an unequal status quo by shifting attention away from structural issues.

Whatever the reason, this colorblind approach became increasingly unsustainable. We were forced to concede that our work was not "colorblind," it was racist blind and color silent.[9]

The year 2020 was a breaking point.

IMAGINING A BETTER WAY

We, and the behavioral science field, hummed along, racial blinders snuggly in place, until 2020 changed everything. George Floyd's murder catalyzed a national reckoning, the COVID-19 pandemic disproportionately devastated Black and Brown communities, and the Black Lives Matter protests that spread across the country (and then the world) demanded justice and made it clear that the stakes were nothing less than the survival of entire communities.

For us, this moment cracked open a space to imagine and push for a better way in our work and field. And it revealed the stakes: the promise of applied behavioral science to improve lives will remain unrealized until we acknowledge and address racist institutions, practices, and systems.

The historian, professor, and antiracism activist Ibram X. Kendi makes a powerful argument about the way policies can support or fight against the racist status quo: "There is no such thing as a nonracist or race-neutral policy. Every policy in every institution in every community in every nation is producing or sustaining either racial inequity or equity between racial groups."[10]

As behavioral science's influence has reached into the corridors of policy and extended into people's daily lives, so has the responsibility of its practitioners, teachers, students, and even fans to make sure that our work is not "race neutral" or "colorblind" in theory and rac*ist* blind in practice. We should not be the people poet Nayyirah Waheed was referring to when she said "never trust anyone who says they do not see color. This means to them, you are invisible."[11] We should aim to practice antiracist behavioral science.[12]

First, what do we mean by colorblind or race neutral? Take a "straightforward" voting law that everyone must produce a driver's license to vote. While on the surface this law seems to have nothing to do with race, systemic racism plays its part, snaking beneath the surface, influencing behavior.

As recently as 2020, people who identified as Black, Latino, or Native American were about twice as likely as those who identified as white to lack a nonexpired government-issued photo ID.[13] Excluding people without an ID from voting disproportionately hurts BIPOC. Not surprisingly, several studies have found that photo ID laws decrease election day turnout among BIPOC.[14] In a country where a tiny slice of votes can determine the seats of power, this ostensibly "race-neutral" policy potentially disenfranchises people of color and preserves power within the white majority.

Questioning the idea of race-neutral policies should come naturally to behavioral scientists. As a field, we've embraced a similar idea: there are no "behaviorally neutral" programs or policies. Think of the classic "where to place the apples in a cafeteria" example in the popular book *Nudge*. If you run a cafeteria, you must make decisions about where to put all the food. Because people are influenced by convenience, placing apples in attractive, prominent locations influences them to eat more apples, nudging people toward healthier choices. But you could also put candy bars in the prime spot and apples in a less visible place. Now you're steering people toward cavities!

Because we are influenced by even small situational factors, decisions about how a policy or program is designed is consequential, not neutral. When we recognize this as a field, we acknowledge that constant unseen forces influence behavior, and our interventions can either sustain a harmful status quo (keep the candy) or push against it (replace the candy with apples).

It's time to extend this line of reasoning and acknowledge the larger situational factors that disproportionately affect Black and Brown people in America: racism is pervasive and influences every facet of life. Failing to account for this endemic situational factor could be undermining the impact of our field. More urgently, if our interventions are simply applied on top of long-standing structural inequities, we inadvertently reinforce those racist practices and policies.

Indeed, building on Kendi's work, we define the racist application of behavioral science as any intervention that directly or indirectly produces or sustains racial inequity between racial groups. Imagine an intervention to improve maternal health outcomes. A traditional approach would consider possible cognitive, not structural, biases. For example, attending prenatal appointments increases the chances of a healthy pregnancy, but research has shown that actions that must be repeated can feel like a hassle and therefore drop off over time. So, an intervention might send women text message reminders about upcoming appointments.

While research teams might think about how to improve maternal health outcomes for those living in poverty broadly, it's very unlikely the intervention would acknowledge that BIPOC women and their babies are more likely to die during pregnancy and childbirth than white women and their babies. The resulting "colorblind" intervention might consider income-level barriers like health-care access. And so the text message reminders might also include tips on accessing federal benefits like Medicaid.

But health-care access is the result of deeper historical, systemic, and political forces that were specifically designed to discriminate against Black and Brown people. As BIPOC scholar Joia Crear-Perry, a physician and policy expert, put it, "race is not a factor for illness and death, but racism, bias, and discrimination definitely are."[15]

With this lens, we can see that access to health care is only one barrier—the quality of that care matters too. In fact, research has shown that issues like interactions between women and their health-care providers, including disrespect, disparaging comments, and dismissing Black women's pain, may help explain why Black women are more likely to die of pregnancy complications at every income level. And it may explain why death rates for infants born to Black women with advanced degrees are higher than rates for babies born to white mothers who didn't finish high school.[16]

Because our theoretical intervention wasn't designed to acknowledge, understand, or address any of these deeper barriers faced by BIPOC women, it's reasonable the intervention might have some effect on white women while failing to address the larger barriers faced by women of color. The vast majority of studies in our field are not disaggregated by race and ethnicity,[17] so the results of our hypothetical intervention would only name the *average* impact on women in the study. Eventually, the results might be summarized as something like "Text Message Reminders Increase Positive Health Impacts for Women." Beneath that headline would be a community whose racist-imposed barriers persist, untouched and unacknowledged. In Kendi's framing, this well-meaning intervention has sustained racial inequity between racial groups.

We can do better. Again, inspired by Kendi, we define an antiracist application of behavioral science as interventions designed to identify or quantify racial inequities and/or to produce or sustain racial equity between racial groups. Antiracist application of behavioral science means actively examining racism by asking, What role does (or could) racism play in this context?

Let's revisit the maternal health intervention now with an antiracist lens. In a reimagined design stage, researchers would identify the elevated risks BIPOC women face and work to identify the underlying causes, including structural biases. Research teams would reach out to sister disciplines like public health to draw from successful interventions that have focused on BIPOC communities.

For instance, studies have found that doulas (trained professionals who offer comprehensive childbirth support) can effectively navigate health-care systems and address biases, especially for Black women and women with low incomes.[18] Doulas seem to "stand in the gap," as one doula put it, of improper treatment by facilitating informed decisions, helping women advocate for themselves and improving interactions with providers. In light of these insights, it's not surprising that BIPOC and low-income women are more likely to report receiving respectful health care and experience significantly lower cesarean and preterm birth rates when they have a doula by their side.[19]

Given this, our revised behavioral intervention might partner with a local doula network to run interventions encouraging women to sign up for doula care. The intervention can reflect both behavioral and antiracist insights. For example, social science tells us that belonging is important. Public health research tells us that "racial concordance"—a shared identity between patient and care providers—matters.[20] And so, outreach to BIPOC mothers might include pictures of BIPOC doulas. Quantitative data would capture the health impacts both on average and on BIPOC women specifically. Qualitative data could capture the experiences of BIPOC women as they navigate the health-care system to identify and amplify any racial disparities in care. Finally, aiming to make upstream improvements, the intervention could follow the example of public health studies in this area (by Katy Kozhimannil and colleagues) by specifically working with women who have Medicaid coverage so that any positive study results can be translated into specific policy implications, like lobbying for Medicaid programs to cover the cost of doula care.[21]

Looping back to Kendi, we would call this revised version an antiracist behavioral intervention because it aimed to identify and quantify racial inequities and to produce racial equity. It doesn't always make sense to examine the role of race and racism as a central consideration—but far too often we don't even ask.

We want to pause here and recognize that for many readers using the term antiracist in this context will seem too muscular or overly ambitious. Or maybe it feels passe—a bit too May 2020. America does seem to have pushed its *How to Be an Antiracist* ambitions into the back of our collective closet (with our now-dusty N95 masks and hand sanitizer). Our tendency to retreat from hard conversations about racism is understandable, but it's also a massive barrier if we sincerely want to understand and improve lives. So we use the term throughout this book. To us, an antiracist approach simply acknowledges that racism exists and responds to that reality with the goal of making things better not worse.

To be clear, we don't believe applied behavioral science can dismantle structural racism on its own, but we've confused our limitations with powerlessness. Behavioral scientists have an opportunity and a responsibility to play a role in bending the "the arc of the moral universe" toward justice.[22]

IS THE NUDGE A FUDGE?

Maybe the field has shied away from seriously examining structural racism because applied behavioral science has focused on applying insights about *individual* biases to help *individuals* make better choices. Many leaders and practitioners in the field are social psychologists who are trained to understand the person in light of their situation. And yet applied behavioral scientists have consistently looked to change the person rather than their situation.

For policymakers, the idea that cheap and easy strategies could address society's problems by "nudging" individual behavior was seductive; it meant avoiding systemic changes and the politically complex battles such change involves. Unsurprisingly, the idea of nudging people via small changes quickly interested powerful leaders. But as the scholars Nick Chater and George Loewenstein lay out in their important paper, relying solely on nudges fails to challenge root causes.[23] They explain that they subscribed to the belief that "many of society's most pressing problems can be addressed cheaply and effectively at the level of the individual, without modifying the system in which the individual operates. We now believe this was a mistake." They quote the writer Frank Pasquale's blunt assessment of the whole endeavor: "the nudge is really a fudge—a way of avoiding the thornier issues at stake."[24] Moreover, the proposed nudges that focused on the individual, they argue, might even cause an erosion of the will to address systemic issues.[25]

Chater and Loewenstein advocate for a new direction, one which we subscribe to: "the most important way behavioral scientists can contribute to public policy is by employing their skills to develop and implement value-creating system-level change." And we agree with them that individual- and policy-level approaches don't have to be mutually exclusive. For example, they note that we can have nudges to stop smoking (like gruesome images on cigarette packages) *and* implement tobacco taxes. However, to be race aware, policymakers and researchers working on the issue should acknowledge and design around the reality that the tobacco industry intentionally targeted Black and Brown communities for decades.

For example, a race-neutral policy might ban most tobacco ads. A race-aware policy (like the plan announced by the Food and Drug Administration

(FDA) in 2021 to ban menthol cigarettes and all characterizing flavors in cigars) would specify that an advertising ban must also include ads for menthol.[26] It would note that menthol cigarettes specifically had been pushed on the Black community for over fifty years—placing more advertising in predominantly Black neighborhoods and publications and intentionally hiring Black influencers to hand out menthols in Black communities.[27]

Working toward antiracist behavioral science is the responsibility of students, academics, practitioners, and even those who are simply interested in the discipline. By leaning into our ambition and optimism to design for the world we want, rather than the one we have, we move the field and fight for justice forward. We want to change the game, not just help individuals be better players.

HOW THIS BOOK (AND YOU) CAN HELP

Engaging in antiracism can feel abstract and aspirational. This book focuses on how organizations, policymakers, and the public can use the tools of behavioral science in practical ways to design and implement policies and practices that drive racial equity forward.

Anyone who has followed the growth of this field will find the strategies outlined in this book useful. It's an actionable companion for students in a range of fields—psychology, business, public policy, and law—who are learning about applied behavioral science. Those who teach and conduct behavioral science research will also find useful tools to use as they integrate social justice engagement into their work.

Policymakers and those practicing behavioral science inside the US federal government will find this book especially useful in responding to President Biden's original Executive Order 13985, "Advancing Racial Equity and Support for Underserved Communities through the Federal Government," which he signed on his first day in office, as well as the updated Executive Order 14091, "Furthering Advancing Racial Equity and Support for Underserved Communities through the Federal Government."[28]

These executive orders charge the federal government with advancing equity, including with communities that have long been underserved, and addressing systemic racism in national policies and programs. Specifically, the updated order calls on agencies to create equity action plans to assess obstacles to racial equity. These plans must acknowledge how federal agency decisions, regulators, and officials contribute to racial inequity and specify how agencies will align their actions to repair those harms. To meet these presidential directives, federal agencies must examine any and all internal racist practices and norms. While they may not have the same order from the president of the United States, applied behavioral science teams outside the government should do the same.

Finally, program and product designers, policymakers, funders, and anyone working in social services should find actionable resources in these pages. For example, consider a volunteer tax preparer who surveys clients and discovers that BIPOC individuals are more likely to discuss their financial goals with a BIPOC preparer, causing them to change their staff recruitment process. Similarly, a city planner might intentionally map neighborhoods by race and income, only to discover that BIPOC majority areas of the city are least likely to have green space, prompting them to thoughtfully shift budgets and building plans to rectify the imbalance. We will examine examples such as these in depth.

The chapters ahead provide a call to action and a pathway forward. Through accessible stories, examples, and practical tools, readers will learn how to practice antiracist behavioral science by reforming our research methods, diversifying the field, and partnering with diverse teams.

Chapters 1 through 3 take readers through an early history of applied behavioral science, discussing "classic" behavioral biases and charting where the field made crucial turns away from tackling systemic issues. Chapter 4 dives into the mechanics of behavioral design and describes the traditional behavioral mapping process and then proposes an updated antiracist framework. Chapter 5 provides stories that illustrate how an antiracist version of the behavioral design process could unfold. Chapters 6 through 11 detail each step in the proposed antiracist behavioral mapping process, and chapter 12 translates our insights, stories, and analyses into specific, actionable steps that critical actors like students, funders, and academics can take to move the field forward.

Finally, a resources section can be found at the end of the book, organized by chapters. In it, we list practical tools, case studies, and articles that we hope will help readers translate insights from this book into practical applications.

Our premise is not original, but we do hope that it reignites a sense of responsibility among our readers. Others have called for social scientists to be more active in the pursuit of racial justice. In the thick of the Civil Rights Movement in 1967, Dr. Martin Luther King, Jr. gave a call to action in a speech to the American Psychological Association (APA) entitled "The Role of the Behavioral Scientist in the Civil Rights Movement": "white society is in even more urgent need [of the social sciences]. . . . to understand that it is poisoned to its soul by racism and the understanding needs to be carefully documented and consequently more difficult to reject."[29] The time to start is now.

URGENT AND POSSIBLE

Now is the time to push the field to a more evidence-based and honest stance on racism, before our current "color silent" habits calcify into hardened standards of practice. In political discourse, "calcification" has been used to describe the phenomenon of policies, practices, and beliefs becoming entrenched, leading to stagnation and resistance to reform. The longer our field overlooks systemic injustices, the more entrenched our practices, templates, and literature become, making it harder for the field to adopt an antiracist approach.

The rise of artificial intelligence (AI) and machine learning raises the stakes. AI systems rely on all available data collected from published papers, surveys, and experiments. If the information fed into the AI system is biased, the system will perpetuate that bias. The presidential executive order mentioned above on further advancing racial equity includes a useful term of the worrisome result: "algorithmic discrimination," which refers to instances when automated systems contribute to racist and unjust treatment based on their actual or perceived identity.

For example, if our studies rely on populations that are predominantly white or male, the AI system may not be able to accurately identify patterns for other demographic groups. More broadly, if the behavioral research fed into AI systems all frame failures to save or take up health insurance (for example) as individual errors while neglecting to mention underlying causes of poverty and unequal access to health care, AI systems may produce biased results and recommendations. The emergence of ChatGPT, Google's Gemini and other AI systems have reignited conversations about how racism manifests in AI systems, perpetuating injustice.

Even AI systems designed to be "race blind" can perpetuate racial bias. A recent study and subsequent Internal Revenue Service (IRS) internal investigation is a useful example.[30] Researchers working with the US Treasury Department discovered that Black taxpayers accounted for 21 percent of Earned Income Tax Credit (EITC) claims but were the focus of 43 percent of EITC audits.[31] The heart of this inequity was in the way the IRS algorithm has been flagging potential audits.

The good news is that just as humans constructed unjust systems, we also have the power to dismantle them. Uncovering the biased AI systems used by the IRS was made possible in part because President Biden's executive order gave economists at the Treasury Department the motivation to dig into the issue. The tax filers' demographic data wasn't available, but researchers were innovative and estimated race data based on taxpayer names and neighborhood demographics. The IRS followed up with an internal study of its own and has committed to correct the issue.[32] Applied behavioral science should be at least as progressive as the IRS.

As we write this, a noisy argument is taking place in America. Conservatives attack a "woke agenda" as progressives attempt to push the nation into recognizing systemic injustices. It's sometimes a useful conversation (and sometimes a shouting match), but this book isn't meant to tackle it. Instead, our goal is to uncover the ways our field has overlooked specific cases of racial injustices, demonstrate how that oversight harms our science, and provide a practical guide on a better way forward.

As we do so, we will make mistakes—including in the very pages of this book. We will use blurry, imprecise words word like "equality" when we very specifically mean racial justice. Despite our best efforts, we'll sometimes fail to use systems-centered language. Our future behavioral interventions will not always be perfect models of antiracism in action. Perfection is not the point, and it has kept many well-intentioned people from rolling up their sleeves and trying to integrate racial justice into their work.

We love this field. We are proud that we have each devoted our careers to research, practice, and teaching and service in the behavioral science community. We aren't the first, or the only scholars in this field, to call for deep changes. We stand with and learn from these colleagues and hope that this book will be a resource for anyone who wants to design programs, policies, or products that aim to make the world a better, more just place.

I THE PROMISE AND FUNDAMENTAL FLAW OF APPLIED BEHAVIORAL SCIENCE

1 APPLIED BEHAVIORAL SCIENCE: KEY INSIGHTS AND CRITICAL OVERSIGHTS

> Not one of us was here when this house was built. Our immediate ancestors may have had nothing to do with it, but here we are, the current occupants of a property with stress cracks and bowed walls and fissures built into the foundation. We are the heirs to whatever is right or wrong with it. We did not erect the uneven pillars or joists, but they are ours to deal with now.
>
> —ISABEL WILKERSON

We want to dive into the ways behavioral science has been braided into our lives and the ways it unintentionally overlooks and affirms racist structures. But first, let's step back and unravel the backstory to examine how and why these techniques took off in the first place. Like finding our way when we're lost, we'll retrace our steps to identify early wrong turns and overlooked side roads. By doing so, we can determine where we need to change course and map out a better way forward.

Theories of behavioral science grew, in large part, to present a more nuanced and recognizable model of human behavior than the one presented by traditional neoclassical economic theory: humans are rational actors who make decisions to maximize utility.

Early behavioral economists and psychologists stepped back, looked at this assumption, and asked, essentially, Wait, what? Who *really* acts this way?

Let's look more closely: *we are rational actors maximizing utility*. If we truly maximize, then a lack of retirement savings wouldn't be a national issue in the United States. According to this theory, we would all be putting small amounts from our paychecks into our retirement accounts today because we know we will need it later. (Demonstrably false.[1]) There would not, at recent accounting, be millions of "left-behind or forgotten" US retirement accounts, holding approximately $1.65 trillion[2] (!) in assets because forgetting money that you went to the effort of actually saving is pretty much the opposite of profit maximizing.[3] Everyone who needs it would sign up for free prescription drugs even if the process is complicated and frustrating. (Also false.) Finally, we would not stay up late watching *The Last of Us* when we know we'll be exhausted, grumpy, and unproductive the next day (Mindy's first-person experience confirms this is also false).

More to the point of this book (even if these early behavioral economists weren't talking about it), race-based hiring discrimination[4] wouldn't be an issue because corporations and agents would never intentionally shrink the labor pool, driving wages up and minimizing utility and profits. Or take redlining,[5] which explicitly prohibited loans to Black people and other people of color, by outlining (in red) areas with sizable Black populations as a warning to mortgage lenders. Traditional economic theory deems limiting access to capital based not on risk but on skin color irrational since it harms the economy at large, increasing the possibility of economic stagnation and unemployment for everyone, not just the excluded group.[6]

Academics began to test drive the rational actor theory through empirical and theoretical experiments and in the process began to document predictable "deviations" from the rational actor model. Their work merged insights from psychology (both social and cognitive psychology) and economics. In lab experiments, researchers identified and quantified these behavioral deviations, which came to be commonly known as heuristics and biases—shortcuts we use to navigate a complex world. Despite a reliance on relatively homogenous (white and formally educated) study populations, this early research unearthed rich (and at the time, radical) insights about behavior. These studies laid the foundation for the field, though many of the findings were unearthed in rarefied lab settings.

Early behavioral science research demonstrated the specific ways that we humans are not perfect rational actors humming through complex calculations with precision but instead more like a computer with too many tabs open—overloaded with information and trying to keep up. The scientific term for this is *bounded rationality*.[7] It's the concept that mental bandwidth (and thus, pure rationality) is limited when people engage in decision-making. As a result, it's impossible to find the "optimal" option in most contexts. We rely on heuristics (shortcuts) we've developed to make quick decisions in a complex world. More importantly, we're more likely to make errors (or rely on a mental shortcut) when we lack important resources such as time or money.[8]

For example, imagine a hungry, cash-strapped student who is trying to eat healthfully. She's looking at a menu and thinking about what options are healthy, delicious, cheap, and filling. A salad: healthy but not particularly filling or delicious. Philly cheesesteak: delicious and filling but not healthy. Sushi: both healthy and delicious but too expensive. Because reality demands that she make a decision (people are waiting and the cashier looks annoyed), her limited bandwidth leads to the development of mental shortcuts that simplify the choice. She suddenly notices a small sticker on a menu item that says "most popular healthy choice." She quickly scans the price, stops calculating, and points to that item.

Nobel Prize-winning psychologist Daniel Kahneman lays out a closely related framework in his essential book *Thinking, Fast and Slow*. Kahneman describes "System 1" versus "System 2" mental processes.[9] System 1 modes of thinking and processing operate very quickly, rely on emotion and instinct, and tend to require little mental bandwidth. Think of our student using the "most popular" sticker as a shortcut to her decision. By contrast, System 2 modes of thought are slower, more logical, and deliberate. Think of the mechanics your mind uses to work out a difficult math problem.

While it may seem like System 2 is the ideal way of thinking, this isn't quite true. Patterns and heuristics developed thanks to System 1 can lead us astray, for sure, but they also enable us to function in the context-rich social environments that would otherwise overwhelm System 2. In the TV show *The Good Place*, this idea is embodied in the character of Chidi, whose attempt to weigh all evidence before making any decisions paralyzes him and frustrates everyone in his life. As he says after agonizing over which muffin to choose for a snack: "OK, I've made a decision . . . I want to start crying."

And then he starts crying. System 1 helps us avoid this level of anxiety and paralysis and more comfortably navigate the world, but it does so by leaning on mental shortcuts or biases.

THREE BEHAVIORAL BIASES

Over the years, researchers have identified dozens of behavioral biases—far too many to detail in depth here. To provide a brief illustration, we describe three insights that have become regularly used in designing interventions as behavioral science has gained wider application.[10] These include complexity avoidance, present bias, and social influence.

Complexity avoidance recognizes that while people seek to maximize profit or financial gain (in line with the predictions of rational actor theories), they also want to maximize ease.[11] This can often result in avoiding even moderately complex tasks. Experimental evidence shows that people are generally less likely to choose an option as its complexity (as compared to other options) increases and will avoid or put off complex choices all together.

For example, if people were utility maximizing, they would register for a free prescription drug plan even if the sign-up process is complicated. However, this does not bear out, putting a point in the behavioral economists' column versus the rational actor theory. The Medicare Part D rollout was intended to provide better prescription coverage for Medicare beneficiaries, but its 2006 launch was fraught with confusion.[12] For example, imagine an average elderly couple in 2006. (As a reminder, 2006 was still early internet. MySpace was the most visited website that year.[13]) Using websites for benefit enrollment is relatively new, and the couple is put off by the technology. Accessing the site is confusing, and once there, they see multiple plans, each with different monthly costs and benefits. It's overwhelming. They don't "decide" to forgo prescription drug coverage forever, but they do put it off indefinitely, which is the same thing. Our elderly couple is not fictional. Many people at the time found it too difficult to understand their eligibility and the web of various costs and benefits. A common response was to avoid making an active choice, even if that meant going without health insurance!

The technique of simplification can be used to overcome this bias. By streamlining a multistep process or one that involves many options, complexity is reduced, making it more likely that decisions will be made instead of avoided. Another approach is to provide individuals with decision-making support. In the prescription drug example, providing families with tools to distill the most salient aspects of the choice might help them align with their goals and make a choice. For example, imagine being able to sort plans by cost and underlying condition, or adding a benefit calculator that gives plans a grade depending on your personal information.

In one classic example, behavioral scientists considered insights around simplification to improve application rates for the US Free Application for Federal Student Aid (FAFSA). Researchers found that providing families with support in completing the FAFSA forms (simplifying the process, not only providing information) was a route to higher rates of form completion and access to financial aid.[14] We will revisit this study, with a critical eye toward antiracism, but in this context, it should be celebrated as an effective demonstration of how to address complexity avoidance.

Present bias describes our tendency to value payoffs that are closer to the present moment more than payoffs in the future.[15] For example, if given the choice between receiving $10 today versus $15 tomorrow, most people choose $10 today. We can't wait. But now imagine you're given the choice between receiving $10 in a year or $15 in a year and one day. Well, in a year and a day we somehow will be better, more patient people. When the time horizon is pushed forward, most people say that they can wait for the higher reward.

In behavioral science terms, people are showing "time-inconsistent preferences." We all do this, to some degree, and it's possible some people exhibit more inconsistency than others. For example, one study has shown that individuals who choose to drive under the influence of alcohol are more likely to hold time-inconsistent preferences. In other words, the desire to get home *now* (for free, and under my own power) outweighs my preferences for the *future* (getting home safely and avoiding a fine, accident, or worse).

To address present bias, one strategy is to give decision makers information about their progress toward their goals—making the goal and the future more salient. Tracking incremental progress can decrease the psychological distance between the present state and some goal (e.g., saving for a vacation or paying down a credit card). There are plenty of phone apps that allow users to set and achieve a long-term goal by providing present-based rewards like points or starts, to keep people on track. To understand this idea, consider an intervention that does the opposite: any opportunity to "buy now and pay later" makes it easy for someone to prioritize their feelings in the present (enjoying a shiny new toy) and allows them to avoid thinking about their future state (a bit more debt).

Finally, **social influence** describes the process in which people, as social animals, take the behavior of others as a cue to how we ought to behave. For example, imagine you're walking in a new city attempting to cross an empty street. The most important and consequential message you will receive is not the "official" stop or walk sign but rather a quick glance around to see what others are doing. If others walk breezily against the stop walking sign, you will very likely hop off the curb and follow. Researchers have repeatedly found that we're especially influenced by those we perceive as similar to ourselves.

Social science research has repeatedly demonstrated the impact of social comparison and its influence on behavior, an idea called "social proof." Providing people with information about how their behavior compares to others can instigate social comparison, which in turn may impact behavior in prosocial domains like voting, littering, and energy consumption.[16] In other areas, people may simply look to others to see what behaviors or options might be the best fit. The couple choosing between a prescription drug plan may ask their neighbors about their own choices, and this information may help them brush past the webs of complexity to simply do what their neighbors are doing.

In hotels, consumers are more likely to reuse their bath towel (saving a bit of water) when a sign informs them that most hotel guests do the same.[17] People are also less likely to drop litter in a pristine space as compared to a messy space—in this case they're influenced by the *evidence* of what other people have done.[18] For situations that are a bit more ambiguous, the impacts of others' behavior can be even stronger. For example, even though viewers report that canned laughter is annoying and distracting, they still rate TV shows that use canned laughter at key moments funnier than those that do not.[19]

The idea that people predictably react in certain ways is central to the practical application of insights from the field. This neat and simplified framing of humans as predictable creatures helped open the door to designing behaviorally informed interventions. If we can predict errors and inconsistencies, we can design interventions to help address them.

But what if our mistakes are instead dependent on situational constraints and systemic barriers? Suddenly, behavioral interventions become complex, costly, time-consuming, and potentially threatening to white-centered power structures. These are all things that a young field struggling for relevance, funding, and policymakers' approval wants to avoid.

Reflecting on these early days of research and scholarship, we can see that there are at least four specific oversights that the field made (present company included!): a myopic focus on the individual, an underreliance on social psychology, a lack of diverse racial and ethnic representation in our study samples and on our research teams. These errors were the seeds of mistakes that would ripen and bear tainted fruit over time. Perhaps we didn't catch them earlier because they blend in so well with dominant norms of social and psychological science of centering white researchers, white study populations and white perspectives. Our oversights weren't intentional, but as we will describe, they were consequential. Identifying and acknowledging these oversights is a critical first step forward.

WE BLAMED THE PLAYER, NOT THE GAME

The field tends to frame behavioral challenges as individual challenges that arise because of our cognitive limitations. Many of the most important books in this field (such as *Nudge*) spend significant time unpacking the seemingly self-destructive ways individuals make errors in judgement. Larger systemic issues—like structural racism—are almost always ignored.

The term *responsibilization* has been coined in the field of consumer research to describe the process of shifting responsibility from the state and corporations to the "responsible consumer."[20] So, for example, the responsibility of responding to the climate emergency would fall solely on individual consumers to "go on a carbon diet" rather than placing accountability on state and corporate actors by demanding a carbon tax on corporate profits.

In the context of race, our field's use of this individual framing is especially problematic. For example, years of work (including our own) to increase the savings of people living in poverty essentially responds to the challenge of closing the wealth gap by designing interventions to help low-income BIPOC individuals demonstrate greater financial willpower. These studies do not name or attempt to hold accountable racist policies that have systematically denied loans, access to homeownership, quality education, and employment opportunities to people of color.

What if instead the field saw the "responsible consumer" as mythical as the "rational actor"? How would we approach systemic problems differently? Nick Chater and George Loewenstein explored this question in their (previously mentioned) article in which they argue that "the real problem lies not in human fallibility, but in institutions, laws, and regulations that render such fallibility largely irrelevant." We agree, but we also don't think it's that simple. As other key figures in the field, like Michael Hallsworth (managing director of the US-based Behavioural Insights Team), have stated in response to Chater and Loewenstein, the goal of behavioral public policy has not been to avoid policy actions but instead to "integrate behavioral science into existing policy approaches."[21]

We agree that the goal of most applied behavioral scientists—especially those placed in government agencies—is to apply behavioral insights to policy solutions. But we know Hallsworth is right when he admits that "there are definitely fewer clear examples of behavioral science directly producing systemic policy solutions." Indeed, while we've added behavioral insights to the ways in which existing policies are implemented on the margins (e.g., modifying communication to make it easier for families to access public benefits), in our combined experience, we have never worked on a project that was empowered with the ability to create a new or different policy.

More to the point of this book, despite dozens of projects in the United States involving BIPOC populations, we have rarely been part of projects that attempted to even name the larger structural issues of race in which these individuals were making decisions, never mind attempting to push against or change those structures. And just to underline, we worked on projects in cities like DC and Detroit with majority BIPOC populations on issues like poverty, health, and education that definitely and obviously intersected with historical and political racist structures.

Because the field framed societal problems as the result of individual weakness, our solutions focused on fixing individual behavior. This framing is problematic in general, but it is particularly harmful in its application in the United States, where—due to our history and failure to learn from it—racism is an enduring and defining situational factor, rigging who has access to wealth, education, and power. We've been helping people play a game better without acknowledging that the game has been intentionally rigged against people of color.

In behavioral science speak, we would call this tactic "framing."[22] In everyday jargon we could use the same word slightly differently: we "framed" the individual for acts they alone didn't commit. Frames both highlight and obscure. In the case of applied behavioral science, our frame spotlighted individual actors and obscured the role of institutions, allowing unjust norms, practices, and patterns to pass by without critical examination or an opportunity to dismantle them.

We want to bring the stage lights up to encompass systemic injustices, racist policies, and historical discrimination and corresponding privilege that is the backdrop (the situation) BIPOC and white Americans constantly navigate. By looking at race and racism in particular, we can use behavioral science tools to examine, identify, quantify, and work toward dismantling these damaging structures.

WHY WE KNOW MOZART, BUT NOT HIS SISTER

A second and connected major oversight in the application of behavioral insights is an underreliance on theories and findings from social psychology. While cognitive psychology studies the limitation *within* the brain, social psychology examines the impact of *other* people (real or imagined) on our judgment, emotions, and behaviors. Social psychology allows for more focus on the underlying sociocultural dynamics, which could help us tell a bigger and more accurate story of why humans behave the way we do.

For example, Crystal's situation changed dramatically in the sixth grade when her family moved from a mostly Black to a mostly white neighborhood. She didn't have another Black teacher until college or possibly graduate school. This made her feel like she stood out, making her very self-conscious and worried about how others perceived her (a typical example of what psychologists call stereotype threat). But the white kids in her classes also experienced an impactful situation change: they had a Black kid in their class. Through the rest of her school years, Crystal was almost always the only Black person in her classes and remembers well-meaning teachers pointing out her difference as a lesson to her peers. "We have Crystal here, and she has a different skin color, but we love her just as much as everyone else," they'd say. These sentiments, without fail, made her want to shrink into her desk. Crystal was not by nature a shrinking person, but her situation changed, which influenced her behavior (wanting to shrink).

One crucial insight into human decision-making—particularly relevant to the study of racism—is the power of the situation, which is a fundamental tenet of social psychology. Situationism is the theory that human behavior is driven more by the situation in which we find ourselves rather than by our personal traits. Recall our college student trying to pick a healthy, delicious, and affordable lunch. How would her decision-making be different if the line were long and unruly, and she felt rushed? What if the coffee shop were empty, and she felt no time pressure? Perhaps it would look different again if she were the only Black woman surrounded by a group of white customers?

John Darley and Daniel Batson's research on bystander intervention provides a timeless example of the power of social context. In one of the most important studies in the field, seminary students were asked to prepare a (last-minute) sermon on the biblical story of the Good Samaritan and then to walk across campus to deliver it. The question? Which seminarians would stop to help a person (actually a collaborator in the study) hunched in a doorway asking for help.[23] The set-up of the experiment cleverly controlled for common ideas of why people behave the way they do to isolate the power of the situation:

Perhaps people need *motivation* to do good? The researchers purposely chose seminary students from a population that, by definition, has publicly committed to acts of service.

Perhaps people need *information to do good*? Again, the study was set up so that each seminarian had read and prepared a speech on being a Good Samaritan.

These folks were uniformly motivated and informed.

The trick? The situation was manipulated. Half of the seminarians were told they were late to give the talk and had to rush, while the other half was told they were early and had plenty of time to walk across campus. The results: those in a hurry were less likely to stop and offer help to a stranger in a potential emergency than those who thought they had more time.

The findings of this study provide evidence of the often sharp contrast between our disposition (personality, motivations, information) and the situations in which we find ourselves. In this case, people who were motivated and informed were still heavily influenced by their situation (experiencing time pressure or not). One could easily imagine conducting this study with additional layers: would the student be more or less likely to stop if the student were a man and the person in the doorway was a woman? What if the student were white and the person in the doorway were Black? Our situation can act like glasses that influence how we interact with the world, and yet we usually don't realize that we, and everyone around us, are wearing them. When biases like present bias or complexity avoidance are examined on their own, it's easy to overlook influential situational features that can create a more nuanced understanding of the biases.[24]

In many ways, as behavioral science applied its insights to real problems, we fell into a cognitive trap that our field itself had named: the fundamental attribution error. This bias (also known as correspondence bias) says that instead of adequately considering situational factors, we're likely to overattribute behavior to an individual's disposition or personality. In other words, we tend to overemphasize the impact of personal characteristics and underemphasize factors that stem from social context.

For example, Wolfgang Amadeus Mozart is recognized as a musical genius and child prodigy. But few also know that his mother was a singer and his father was an accomplished musician and teacher. His father taught his older sister, Maria Anna, to play piano when she was eight. Her younger brother was often at her side. Instead of waiting until he was eight, his father began lessons when Mozart was only three. Some experts believe this early start helped rewire his brain and accentuate his natural abilities. Maria Anna would later tour with, teach, and support Mozart, along with their father. We attribute Mozart's success to his individual gifts, overlooking that he had two dedicated teachers who were musical masters themselves.

When Maria Anna was only twelve, she toured Europe with Mozart and was called "virtuosic," "a prodigy," and "genius." But while Mozart continued to play on increasingly bigger stages, her musical career was cut short once she was eligible to marry. She and her brother may have had similar individual gifts, but Maria Anna's path to greatness was circumscribed by her situation, while Mozart's was enhanced by his.[25] When we focus on the individual, we miss the ways societal forces like bias shape people's lives.

The prominent social psychologist Claude Steele perfectly captures this oversight in his response to an interview with the organizational psychologist and author Adam Grant in his TED podcast, *ReThinking*.[26] Grant asked Steele, "from all your expertise, is there a piece of advice that's often given that you think is wrong?" Steele responded, "This will sound controversial a bit . . . I think we over stress the power of the individual against the circumstances of life, the contingencies that one has to contend with . . . we overinterpret the power of the individual as they move through their life against circumstance . . . we fall in love with the idea of grit . . . you have to have that, but we over-love it. We love it because it gives us psychologically control over things. . . . But as a society we need to get more mature. We can't rely on that [grit] to have a fair society."

Steele goes on to advise that "we need to be much more sensitive to the circumstances, conditions and kind of threats people are under if we are going to move forward. I see that as something I'd like to see as a bigger part of our future as a society and maybe even as a civilization." His work provides us with an example of how to consider the impact of bias and discrimination on behavior, and how to design policies and programs that mitigate its impact. Steele, who is Black, is best known for his work on stereotype threat, a situation where individuals perceive a risk of conforming or demonstrating stereotypes about a group to which they belong.

The first experiments demonstrating stereotype threat were conducted by Steele and Joshua Aronson[27] and showed that Black students performed worse on a tricky portion of the Graduate Record Examination (GRE) when the test was framed as being "diagnostic of intellectual ability." This language evoked the negative stereotype that Black people were less intellectually capable. But the performance dip disappeared when the same test was framed as nondiagnostic of ability. In Steele and Aronson's study, the Black students seemed to internalize the fear of confirming the negative belief that they would be less capable of performing in an intellectual exercise. Their important research led to many insights about how to avoid or reduce this phenomenon. For example, strategies like providing sufficient role models and emphasizing the role of motivation and effort have been shown to increase performance in situations that might otherwise be psychologically threatening.

WEIRD REPRESENTATION

The final two oversights are closely related: many behavioral insights come from lab studies that use homogenous populations, and as a result, many behavioral interventions are based on original research that consists of relatively privileged groups of people. Specifically, they rely on populations that are largely white and, as they have come to called WEIRD: Western, Educated, Industrialized, Rich, and Democratic.[28] Studies have shown that even though only 5 percent of humans live in WEIRD settings, approximately 96 percent of studies in the top psychology journals use these populations.[29] A widespread reliance on insights from these WEIRD populations may be inadvertently limiting the potential effectiveness of our interventions.

Finally, our research teams—then and now—suffer from underrepresentation of BIPOC voices. In 2003, Black and Latino researchers accounted for just 4 percent and 3 percent of the workforce in behavioral and social sciences research, respectively. Ten years later in 2013, representation had only risen by a single percentage point.[30] We've felt this personally. Despite engaging in dozens of projects that have involved BIPOC populations, we have hardly ever worked with other Black, Latino/a, or mixed-race scholars.

This matters because when BIPOC representation increases, you have more people in a room who can identify invisible but pivotal situational barriers. Imagine a group working on understanding what makes it hard for low-income BIPOC students to repay loans. A group that is entirely white and well-off may focus on what their training has taught them—can we decrease hassles in the repayment process? Are reminders needed? On the other hand, those with firsthand experience might point out a situation that is more common among BIPOC college students: while in college they were also sending money to their parents. They might also note that not all cash outflows are obvious; some might feel embarrassing. But when there are too few people representing a group, it can be lonely and difficult to share what feels like an outsider's perspective. As social science itself has shown, it's hard and uncomfortable to be the lone dissenter in a group.

The field's early oversights went largely unnoticed, and the first few years of research seemed rich, exciting, and able to demonstrate that behavioral insights could create meaningful change with small tweaks. But the reality is that the stickiest policy issues require a focus on individual behavior *and* structures and institutions.

Perhaps because the field grew so fast, we didn't take time to pause and question whether we were responsibly applying our theoretical insights. And before we knew it, our ideas had launched into the world.

2 WHAT'S AT STAKE AND WHAT'S POSSIBLE

> An America that looks away is ignoring not just the sins of the past but the sins of the present and the certain sins of the future.
>
> —TA-NEHISI COATES

The early successes in demonstrating the ways people veer from previously accepted "rational actor" models brought behavioral science into everyday conversation. Policymakers were especially excited by the field's potential to create big impacts with small changes. A handful of applied examples would be repeatedly held up to demonstrate the science's ability to make good on this lofty promise.

For example, Richard Thaler and Schlomo Benartzi designed the Save More Tomorrow intervention in 2004 to increase retirement savings.[1] Their groundbreaking approach helped people avoid present bias and loss aversion by allowing them to make a commitment *now* to save in the future, linking their savings to future pay raises. Once enrolled in the program, workers continue participation until they opt out. This approach was included as a part of the 2006 Pension Protection Act and has been estimated to have helped more than fifteen million people in the United States increase their retirement savings.[2]

Similarly, Opower, an American company founded in 2007 by Dan Yates and Alex Laskey, used behavioral science insights in the utility space. The founders' approach used social proof to promote individual energy efficiency behaviors. By providing utility customers information about their energy usage relative to others in their neighborhood, they induced behavior change within households, leading to more energy conservation.[3] The intervention had large and exciting impacts that were explored by other scholars like Hunt Allcott and Todd Rogers.[4] Opower was later purchased by Oracle and has now worked with more than one hundred utility companies and served tens of millions of customers worldwide.[5]

These studies applied behavioral insights to high-profile social issues, and their results excited policymakers. Excitement translated into investment and gave behavioral science an influential seat at the policymaking table. One such development was the establishment of the first BIT in the United Kingdom, unofficially referred to as the Nudge Unit, in 2010. The BIT was set up within the UK Cabinet Office with the goal of generating and applying behavioral insights to public policies and services.[6]

Countries like Australia, Germany, the Netherlands, Singapore, and the United States soon followed, setting up their own behavioral insight units within their central governments. In the United States, a 2015 executive order directed federal agencies to incorporate behavioral science into their programs.[7] These units tackled the most fundamental social issues of the day. According to a 2017 analysis of the behavioral units in the United States and the United Kingdom, issues tackled included financial security, education, job training, energy use, health, fraud, debt, illegal migration, theft, and online exploitation.[8] According to the Organisation for Economic Co-operation and Development, there are hundreds of institutions around the world applying behavioral insights to public policy. Many of them coordinate to share best practices and lessons learned among policymakers.[9]

THE ELUSIVE PROMISE OF BIG IMPACTS WITH SMALL CHANGES

Studies like Save More Tomorrow and OPower applied behavioral insights to real-world problems, and their impacts are impressive. But after more than twenty years of application, it's now clear that pointing to these as *illustrative* of the type of impacts the field could achieve is like pointing to Simone Biles as illustrative of what good gymnastics looks like. She's the exception, executing maneuvers few other gymnasts even try. Similarly, these studies were almost singularly and extraordinarily successful. Most behavioral interventions result in impacts that are far more modest or have far less scalability than these superstar studies might lead you to believe.[10]

One important reason for the modest results of most behavioral interventions is that most don't address larger structural issues, where the massive benefits would be found. As others have noted, systemic issues in America (e.g., a public educational system dependent on local wealth and taxation for funding, racist lending practices, a justice system that has targeted Black and Brown people) were often the primary cause of the issues we worked on.[11] And if structural issues were the root cause, then interventions aimed at those roots should have been prioritized—or at least considered.[12] Instead, we focused on the symptoms.

We see this clearly because we're both guilty of overlooking systemic roots of inequity and focusing on symptoms, especially in our early work in the field.

WHEN SHOCKS AREN'T SHOCKING

We were both lucky to be involved in the exciting early days when behavioral insights were just being applied to real-world challenges. Crystal served as an advisor to the US Department of Health and Human Services, and Mindy worked as one of the first employees at ideas42, one of the first, and now largest, behavioral design firms in the world.

After finishing graduate school at Princeton University, we became fast friends and collaborators. As we described in the introduction, our first project was conducted in Philadelphia with Volunteer Income Tax Assistance (VITA) sites, where volunteers help families who qualify complete and file their tax returns for free. Our goal was to convince low-income tax filers to invest a portion of their tax refunds into savings products like 401(k) retirement accounts, 529 education savings accounts, and savings bonds. VITA filers often received significant refunds from the EITC averaging over $2,000 per tax filer. For low-income families, this presents a very sizable cash windfall. We took up the lofty goal of trying to convince tax filers to divert some of their refund to a (relatively nonliquid) savings product.

In theory, focusing on small savings made sense. Sudden "shocks" like a broken car or slipped disc could throw these families into a financial hole too deep to escape. Unable to pay for car repair or doctors' bills, people will lose their jobs, take out risky loans, overdraw their credit cards, and fall deeply into debt and often into bankruptcy. Savings, it was theorized, was a way out.

Mindy remembers thinking of her extended family while working on this project. Their "shocks" weren't "shocking" because they were constant. When income is low, even tiny events are shocks: paying for physical therapy that insurance doesn't cover, wages lost when you have the flu, making dinner for a big family. Credit cards were maxed out, and bills were unpaid. For a decade, Mindy's calls to her extended family would go to the answering machine until she said her name. Only then would the family pick up, assured it was not a debt collector. Against these memories, Mindy imagined her family receiving their EITC refund and encountering a well-meaning nudge to "save" some of it for an emergency. Of course they wanted to save, but their lives were a financial emergency they were constantly managing.

The formation of the "savings at tax time" challenge makes sense for middle- and upper-income folks (those designing the research) whose balance sheet is a steady inflow of income and outflow of expenses. But most of the people we worked with at VITA sites (especially BIPOC families) looked more like each of our extended families: a chaotic stream of debt and financial headaches. As any financial planner will tell you, the best financial decision for people in debt is not to tie up their money in a savings bond but to pay down their mushrooming debt. Saving would be the wrong goal.[13] We ran a few interventions in multiple VITA sites in Philadelphia, but take-up of savings products and services remained extraordinarily low.

About ten years later, Mindy worked with Prosperity Now, a nongovernmental organization (NGO), on a project that aimed to understand clients, not run an intervention. The research was spearheaded by a woman at Prosperity Now who also volunteered as a VITA site manager. Through surveys, site visits, and interviews, we unearthed some relevant insights that helped unpack our earlier experiences in Philadelphia. For example, we found that almost half of VITA clients *did* plan to save but not in the way we had defined and measured it. They intended to (and later reported that they did) put their refunds into a checking or savings account or saved it as cash. They didn't want to save via a savings bond or 401(k) (the focus of most tax-time behavioral interventions then)[14] not because they were "present biased" but because they needed cash to pay daily expenses, and almost half were saving to pay down debt.

None of this is race neutral. In 2016, 60 percent of white families held retirement accounts compared with only 34 percent of Black families and 30 percent of Latino families.[15] This isn't because Blacks and Latinos don't want to save or are more present biased. Structural factors get in the way: among private-sector employees, workers of color are disproportionately represented among those without access to a workplace retirement plan. And debt is not distributed equally: Black and Latino families have a debt-to-assets ratio two to three times higher than that of white families, potentially raising their costs for future borrowing and the probability of defaulting. Again, systemic deprivation and not individual "errors" help explain this debt gap: health-care expenses are one of the primary reasons Americans rack up debt, and that is more likely without access to health insurance, which is more than twice as likely for Latino and Native American households and more likely for Black households.[16] As the economists Darrick Hamilton and William Darity Jr. conclude, "the fact that even a progressive policy such as the EITC does not close the poverty gap by race implies the need for a more comprehensive policy approach."[17]

With the best intentions (and despite our own backgrounds), we came into a situation in Philadelphia we didn't understand well enough and, armed with academic theories that were rich, compelling, and evidence based but detached from many people's lived experiences, we tried to influence how people behaved. This was a mistake that we and our colleagues would make over and over again, on bigger and bigger stages.

BIAS IGNORES BIAS

Our project in Philadelphia was a relatively small pilot made possible by private funding. But a few years later, applied behavioral science had a more prominent role in American policy when the US Department of Health and

Human Services[18] used behavioral science to improve the implementation and efficacy of a set of social service programs that they funded.[19] Crystal served as an academic advisor to the program, which was (in a nod to the field) named BIAS (the Behavioral Interventions to Advance Self-Sufficiency project).

It was an exciting and groundbreaking suite of work, and it represented the first large-scale efforts of a US federal agency to apply behavioral science to the implementation of its programs. Crystal and her colleagues did excellent work. For Crystal, it was exciting to have a seat at the table with those working hard to make these important safety net programs work more effectively. Her excitement (and gratitude) made it easy to ignore some of the deep underlying issues with the approach taken in this work.

Issues of structural racism were never part of the research, even though Black and Latino families are overrepresented in Temporary Assistance for Needy Families (TANF) caseloads, and research suggests they receive unequal services. White TANF recipients are more likely to receive services like childcare, work readiness programs, and education and training. As a result, they have better outcomes, with studies showing that a higher percentage of white recipients without a high school degree who participated in the job readiness program are employed full time compared to similar Black counterparts. The BIAS project ran many meaningful interventions, but these deeper issues were never explored.

THE SBST AVOIDS STRUCTURAL RACISM

In 2013, the application of behavioral sciences would take its largest leap yet in the United States. The Obama administration created the Social and Behavioral Sciences Team (SBST), chaired by the White House Office of Science and Technology Policy (OSTP), to apply behavioral insights across federal agencies. The SBST consisted of policymakers, civil servants from over a dozen government agencies, and behavioral experts, including the two of us.[20] We are both proud to have been a part of this excellent team. But with the power of hindsight, we can see that we missed an enormous opportunity (and platform) to challenge and name racist systems.

For example, Crystal worked on a project with the Department of Education that attempted to address the challenge of identifying students experiencing housing insecurity in public schools. These students have the right to access many support programs, but their teachers and counselors don't often know their status. In the study, an intervention that increased and clarified communication to school staff about these services improved the number of students identified. The result was striking: more than three thousand additional students were potentially reached due to this low-cost intervention. However, an improved study design would have more consciously focused on race (which was *not measured or tracked*) and its intersection with housing insecurity. It was unclear whether this intervention was more effective at reaching a particular profile of students—it wouldn't be unreasonable to assume that white families experiencing housing instability might be more receptive to outreach from a school than families of color. This study design (and lack of follow-up) fails to even speculate on that divergence. We very narrowly focused on one individual touchpoint without adequately considering the broader context.[21]

Two common themes run through our experiences from that small tax site in Philly to our earliest federal work: a focus on individual behavior and failure to name, quantify, or address systemic issues. This oversight was not malicious, but it was consequential. More recently, there has been improvement. Many federal agencies, including the Office of Evaluation Sciences (a team Crystal has worked with often), are attempting to engage with historically oppressed or underserved populations more authentically—but the room for growth is still vast.

FAFSA AND THE OVERLOOKED COLOR OF DEBT

The celebrated behavioral study we mentioned in chapter 1 applied insights regarding complexity avoidance to design a simplified process for applying for college financial aid by prepopulating financial aid forms with already inputted tax data. The intervention resulted in increased FAFSA submissions, increased college applications, and increased college attendance for students with low incomes.[22] Simplifying the FAFSA process would become a popular intervention—tried over half a dozen times since 2009 (including a study by the SBST). At first glance, the results seem unambiguously positive. But when looked at through a race-aware lens, a different picture emerges.

The inspiration for these studies is rooted in the seemingly colorblind—but actually racist blind—narrative that higher education is a path to higher incomes and more wealth for everyone. But as we detailed in the introduction, college-going doesn't pay off, or even translate into, college completion for Black and Latino students as it does for white students. BIPOC students face disadvantages at every step: they are more likely to be targeted for risky (unsubsidized) federal loans,[23] more likely to be targeted by and enroll in expensive for-profit colleges with lower graduation rates,[24] and less likely to have access to help from family in paying off their loans[25] (especially Black women).[26] Moreover, Black and Latino students end up making less despite similar college credentials.[27] The result? Instead of college debt acting as an investment to a brighter future, it can actually push many BIPOC families (and Black families specifically) into a cycle of debt that one policy analyst described as a "low-value debt bomb."[28]

Looking at seven studies that nudged low-income students to complete the FAFSA, we find that all of them failed to acknowledge the racial gap in college completion: most white students graduate within six years, while most Black, Latino, and Native students do not.[29] They also failed to mention that Black college borrowers need to borrow more and are three times more likely to default on their student debt than their white counterparts.

Not surprisingly, given the challenges with loan repayment, Black students are less likely to be able to graduate with a degree. The FAFSA studies also failed to note that for the students who do graduate, the average Black college graduate owes almost 50 percent more than the average white college graduate, and as time goes by, the gap widens, with white college debt decreasing over time and Black debt tripling in four years.[30] Latino and Native American students face similar challenges and higher default rates.[31] Finally, in a field whose stated goal is to help people, not one study noted that Black and Latino borrowers expressed more regret about taking out student loans than their white counterparts.[32] A study surveying Black borrowers reports that more than half have yet to see positive returns on their student loans, which those borrowers now describe as "unpayable," "not worth it," and ultimately like an inescapable burden.

These are consequential impacts for some study participants. But most of the FAFSA studies failed to collect any data on race at all.[33] Those that did specified that the intervention included significant numbers of BIPOC students—meaning that all of the insights above were consequential and relevant to study participants—but did not report downstream impacts by race. Because the interventions were largely successful in increasing FAFSA completion and college attendance, we can assume that these well-meaning studies increased debt among a systematically disadvantaged population without considering the underlying roots, or color of debt. Given everything we know about race and college debt, it's likely (though not yet documented) that a nudge to increase borrowing could have inadvertently increased the number of BIPOC students with debt they're unable to pay off.

As we detail in chapters 5–10, we can do better. For example, this well-publicized research could have taken the opportunity to draw attention to crucial underlying issues: historical employment discrimination and racial wealth gaps often make college unaffordable and loan repayment especially hard for BIPOC populations. Further, researchers could have collected demographic data and followed students from enrollment to graduation, helping to strengthen research on the racialized graduation gap rather than ignoring it. More ambitiously, interventions could be designed to provide additional support for BIPOC students and their families (helping them avoid risky loans and expensive colleges with low graduation rates) to challenge underlying issues. (We explore what could be possible in this study in more detail in chapter 5.)

BIG TOBACCO'S BIG (AND DEADLY) SUCCESS

In contrast to other behavioral interventions in this book that focus on nudging people toward positive behaviors, in this story we explore how the tobacco industry leveraged behavioral insights with an aggressive and explicit focus on race to market menthol cigarettes to Black communities.

Indeed, these efforts have been described as "early behavioral economics" in practice.[34]

Unlike most of our field who still take a colorblind approach to behavior change, in the early 1960s, the big tobacco companies acknowledged and studied race-based segregation to nudge the Black community into smoking menthols. Given all the industry knew at that point about menthol cigarettes' deadly impacts, their aim was predatory and fiendish, but their methods were race aware and highly effective. (In fact, many of their methods are ones we advocate for in this book!) It's no accident that today, nearly nine in ten Black smokers prefer menthol cigarettes.

In 1964, scientific evidence linking smoking to lung and heart disease propelled federal regulators to bar tobacco companies from advertising to their key youth demographic. That meant no advertising on college campuses and no handing out free loose cigarettes to people under twenty-one. In response, the industry pivoted to courting Black smokers, focusing on menthol cigarettes, which are easier to smoke, harder to quit, and more deadly.

To push menthol, the tobacco industry relied on familiar behavioral insights like social proof. Cigarette companies infiltrated Black neighborhoods and recruited community members who interacted with hundreds of others (barbers, bellhops, and taxi drivers) to give out free samples to spread their popularity. Today, we'd call those people "influencers" or "social referents." The industry also capitalized on the marginalization of Black consumers in the United States—creating full-page ads featuring beautiful Black men and women smoking Kools. For a community that rarely saw positive glossy images of themselves, this tactic was likely especially impactful.[35]

Using a research method we'll advocate for later in this book, social scientists working for tobacco companies held focus groups with white- and Black-only participants to understand the desires of each. The researchers learned that "white Chicago" did not want to be seen doing things that "Black Chicago" was doing. So, researchers studied the commuting behavior of Blacks and whites in Chicago to devise an advertising strategy that put menthol cigarette ads on bus routes that Black people took within their segregated neighborhoods. But in bus routes that went through white areas, the ads were only on the inside of the bus so as not to alienate white consumers.

These approaches were incredibly race conscious and successful: by 2020, 86 percent of menthol smokers were Black. The tobacco industry murderously exploited Black communities for profit. Their motives were cruel, but there is a lesson for those of us who seek to uplift and empower: to design effective interventions, we need to acknowledge and study the ways structural injustices manifest in our daily lives.

How can racist structures impact behavioral interventions? As evidenced by the examples above, racist structures show up in at least two concrete ways in behavioral application.

Messengers

First, historical injustices may impact how communities of color respond to messages. Communication from government and other institutional actors may be perceived with skepticism by BIPOC communities, who have had their trust tested (and broken) by American institutions like banks, schools, and police. It is possible that some of the most popular nudges work best when individuals have an existing positive, trusting relationship with an institution or organization. For many folks of color, that trust may not exist. In the case of menthols, big tobacco was aware that messengers wouldn't be race neutral and intentionally recruited Black messengers within the same communities to speak to their targeted Black customers.

Behavioral Maps

Second, the behavioral and institutional barriers BIPOC communities face may be more complex and significant than those that white people face. We start many of our projects by creating behavioral maps, which identify the forces in people's environment that move them toward or away from certain behaviors. These maps help us target where an intervention might help encourage, or discourage, certain behaviors. In chapter 3, we provide two illustrative behavioral maps.

BIPOC communities' behavioral maps feature different, heavier barriers that are not easily nudged to the side. For example, imagine that behavioral scientists were trying to shift people's commuting behavior in Washington, DC from individual car use to less emissions-intensive travel, like biking. Most available research indicates that the lack of protected bike lanes is a major barrier to increased use of bicycles for transport and commuting. So, we can imagine a text message intervention that gives people in DC information about the location of protected bike lanes in their area to encourage them to use a bike instead of a car. This intervention might remove a downstream barrier by making finding protected routes easier, but it doesn't acknowledge or challenge thornier upstream boulders for BIPOC communities, and Black folks especially, like residential segregation or police profiling.

Research that labor economist Charles Brown and colleagues conducted specifically with people who identified as Black, Latino, or mixed suggests "arrested mobility" issues—like fear of police profiling and police violence that impact BIPOC communities, especially men—may also play a significant role in BIPOC's hesitancy to use bike share services. The fear of police violence and profiling is driven by redlining policies that segregated Black neighborhoods and then policed that segregation, often with murderous results. Yet this fear does not appear on a standard survey exploring barriers to biking because this concern is virtually nonexistent for white people.[36]

Or imagine an intervention aiming to decrease smoking among New York City residents. Until recently,[37] in major cities like New York, there were up to ten times more tobacco advertisements in majority Black neighborhoods than in neighborhoods on average.[38] A behavioral map that didn't specifically consider race would miss the forces pressing specifically (and uniquely) on Black people. Because people of color are so severely underrepresented in the behavioral sciences, there may not be anyone designing the intervention with the lived experience to mention that they see menthol ads in every corner of their neighborhood and every page of their favorite magazine.

As it turns out, there are several root causes of the field's disengagement with race and racism. A lack of BIPOC researchers is one of them, but there are additional individual and systemic barriers as well. We explore the most important ones in the next chapter.

3 WHY WE LOOK AWAY, AND WHAT'S POSSIBLE WHEN WE DON'T

> How difficult is it for one body to feel the injustice wheeled at another? Are the tensions, the recognitions, the disappointments, and the failures that exploded in the riots too foreign?
>
> —CLAUDIA RANKINE

If racism is such a consequential aspect of American life and ignoring it diminishes our work, why do we fail to consider race and racism in our research and intervention designs?

We believe there are several important causes: a failure to include BIPOC researchers, a failure to acknowledge and challenge discomfort around race and racism, a lack of professional incentives in tackling this important but difficult subject, and the mistaken view that identifying and aiming to address racist practices is simply "not our job."

A STAGGERING LACK OF RACIAL DIVERSITY

We have not centered the perspective of folks of color in the pursuit of solutions to problems that disproportionately impact them. The continued lack of diversity in academia is staggering—and the social and behavioral sciences are clearly no exception. The behavioral and social science workforce is even less representative of racial and ethnic minorities than biomedical sciences or engineering. Crystal remembers feeling this lack of diversity all too well while she was in university and graduate school. Days before she started undergraduate classes at Carnegie Mellon, a white friend from high school told her that she would be so supported in college because there "weren't very many like her"—meaning talented young Black women ready to study at a competitive school. He genuinely thought he was giving Crystal a compliment and had no idea how hurtful it was. Two decades later, when Crystal attended a Black alumni gathering at her graduate alma mater, Princeton University, she noticed that the group of Black PhD alumni fit into one small room.

We see the lack of diversity in our talent pipeline, and so it's not surprising that influential voices in the field are overwhelmingly white. Journal editors are often the gatekeepers of publication patterns in academia, and the lack of diversity in the field starts upstream. In the psychological sciences, BIPOC scholars remain significantly underrepresented among journal editors, associate editors, and reviewers—over 90 percent of whom are white. This matters because representation makes our work better—good social science is about asking the right questions. But we can't ask what we don't know to ask. One recent study showed that among top-tier psychology journals, only 5 percent focused on race![1] But when BIPOC individuals led journals, the number of published studies examining race nearly tripled.

Our lack of diversity has consequences: in some journals, research conducted by BIPOC scholars (or on predominantly BIPOC samples) is twelve times more likely to be rejected than accepted.[2] Data from the National Institutes of Health (NIH) has shown that (at least when it comes to the NIH)[3] the BIPOC researchers who *are* in the field are less likely to receive funding. The unfortunate result is that insights from BIPOC scholars are less available for applied behavioral science (and the AI systems we will all eventually use) to draw upon. Research also indicates that "racial and ethnic" researchers are more likely to collect more nuanced data on race[4] by, for example, using multiple race-related items rather than a binary variable. Simply put, diverse researchers collect diverse data, and yet as a field, we have failed to fully include BIPOC partners in our work.

DISCOMFORT: A STORY ABOUT BLUNTS

This leads to our second problem: most researchers in applied behavioral science, like most of America, are working from an antiquated definition of racism as bad acts by bad actors rather than as an entrenched system.

When we're trained to be social scientists, our classes focus on theory and quantitative methods. Even if you want to focus on behavior change in the United States, where a third of the population are BIPOC, courses on Indigenous, Latino, African American studies, as well as race theory and similar classes, are almost never offered, let alone required. Our training never asks us to look around and name the racial bias choking America, and we are not taught to catalog its harms. As a result, the field unintentionally relies on the old framework, casting racism as a singular villain twirling his mustache. Unsurprisingly, applied behavioral science has been uncomfortable engaging on issues of race and has no training in dealing with this discomfort.

This can show up differently for BIPOC and whites working in this space. The few BIPOC researchers may be the only ones with lived experience in a room or on a project. It can feel vulnerable and uncomfortable to speak up. We have each felt this acutely, especially early in our careers.

We will forever remember a meeting with collaborators more than a decade ago. One senior member of the team mentioned poverty data he had recently seen that listed cigars as a major expense of Black Americans. One of us noted it would be easy to chalk this up to drug store "blunts" but that spending as a major expense was impossible. The room was silent. Apparently, no one else had ever heard of a blunt or the practice of going down to the nearest drugstore to buy a small cigar to use as a wrapper for a joint. Because rolling papers (at the time) were rarely sold at convenience stores, this practice was common in low-income and majority BIPOC communities. We found ourselves in the humiliating position of having to explain to a group of (stunned and silent) professional colleagues this entire process ("so you have weed but no way to smoke it? But 7-Eleven is nearby?"). When we were done, you could have heard a joint actually drop. Finally, the senior group leader, an economist, broke the silence by shaking his head and declaring, "but that's so inefficient!" It was difficult to speak up, and that discomfort wasn't worthwhile: the new information was greeted with stunned silence, not further questions. There was a palpable desire to move on.[5]

For white people working in the field, talking openly about race and racism can be uncomfortable and even threatening. It's convenient to frame racism as a relic from the past rather than recognizing it as a present system of privilege that affects and implicates even those with good intentions. As the scholar Robin DiAngelo has noted, this type of reflection is particularly difficult for white people. In her influential work, she describes "white fragility" as a state in which any small amount of acknowledgment of racial stress or tension results in defensiveness and denial. This lack of "racial stamina" can make it very difficult for white people to confront (or even acknowledge) the privilege afforded to them.[6] Naturally, this has ramifications for the interventions we design.

"WE DO NOT SAY 'RACE AND CLASS' AT THIS FOUNDATION"

Third, incentive structures in funding and publishing don't support the hard work of confronting racism in our research and designs.

Researchers are faced with limited budgets and constrained timelines, and there are no "bonus" funds for attempting to tackle America's racist past. If anything, there's a disincentive to tackle these issues as race-specific funding is scarce and many researchers are concerned that funders will shy away from funding a barefaced accounting of racist practices. Until recently, these fears were likely well founded.

Many years ago, when Mindy worked for a large foundation focusing on urban education, most of her colleagues were passionate about working to address the racialized opportunity gap in America's schools.[7] However, at the highest levels, specifically naming race was frowned upon. When Mindy gave a talk about the foundation's work, she noted something demonstrably true, "to deal with urban education we must address racism and classism." The foundation required public talks to go through a central approval process. When she submitted the talk, it came back with this section struck out in red marker. The senior communications staff explained bluntly, "we do not say 'race and class' at this foundation."[8] While this was years ago, and funding agencies have since made concerted efforts to improve, there are still few existing funding incentives in the behavioral sciences for taking on this hard and uncomfortable work.

In fact, using five different grant searching tools, we found that the proportion of opportunities dedicated to studying racial equity or systemic racism is close to nonexistent. For example, grant opportunities focused on racial equity and/or structural racism in any way[9] were found in only 1 percent of all funding opportunities listed by the National Science Foundation (NSF) and only 2 percent of all funding opportunities listed by the APA. Further, among funding opportunities listed in relevant NSF divisions, key terms were found in only one grant by the Division of Behavioral and Cognitive Sciences and in *zero* grants by the Division of Social and Economic Sciences.

For academics, publishing incentives for studying the impacts of racism in applied behavioral science are also virtually nonexistent. Journal reviewers and editors privilege research that is perceived to be novel, robust, and universal. As we will discuss later in this book, examining and considering racism in our work often requires more resources, and it can be more difficult to publish the findings. This pattern may be improving (albeit slowly). But while publishing remains the most important currency for hiring and promotion in academia, researchers are incentivized to find the lowest hanging fruit when selecting their research projects. Crystal believes it's no accident that for her, taking a deep dive into questions of race and racism in her research, teaching, and service all developed *after* earning tenure.

A lack of journals in the applied behavioral sciences focused on race contributes to, and is evidence of, our field's failure to explore racism and its effects on behavior. There are very few academic journals that cover both behavioral science and race. We searched large general databases (Scopus and Web of Science), as well as field-specific databases (PsycINFO, EconLit, and Sociological Abstracts), and found that the proportion of journals focused on race or racism[10] was vanishingly small: the average across databases was approximately 0.4 percent.

Interestingly, the journals that did focus on race were only in our sister disciplines. For example, sociology has the *Journal of Race and Class* and the

Du Bois Review—social science research on race. Even economics, often considered to be a conservative discipline, has the *Journal of Economics, Race, and Policy*; the *Review of Black Political Economy*; and the *Journal of Economic Inequality*. Applied behavioral science has zero journals focused on the intersection of race and our science.

Finally, when applied behavioral researchers studying racism do somehow find the funding and a journal in which to publish, there are relatively few field-specific platforms to share their work. Our sister fields have outpaced us. For example, in sociology, there's been the American Sociological Association conference on inequality and structural racism in the United States, the National Conference on Race and Ethnicity in Higher Education (coordinated by the Southwest Center for Human Relations Studies), and the international Sociology of Race and Ethnic Relations Conference. In psychology, there's been the Society for the Psychological Study of Culture, Ethnicity, and Race Research conference and the Decolonizing Psychology Training conference. A similar search using the same key terms ("race," "racial equity," etc.) in behavioral science and behavioral economics turned up only one conference on race by the National Bureau of Economics Research.

So, there is almost no funding to study race and applied behavioral science, and if you do happen to find funding, there are close to zero journals dedicated to publishing that research. And if you do manage to publish, finding dedicated conferences to present your findings or connect with other scholars is equally challenging. For a discipline that studies incentives, we have done a terrible job of setting up an incentive structure that encourages research in this area.

IT'S "NOT OUR JOB"

As a field, we have failed to account for structural racism in our designs and interventions because the challenge feels too big for our tools and methods. While our hesitancy is understandable—applied behavioral science alone won't dismantle structural racism—we have a role to play in the fight toward racial justice. Indeed, some of our most important thinkers, including social psychologists Lee Ross and Richard Nisbett in their classic work *The Person and the Situation: Perspectives of Social Psychology*, have outlined that confronting systemic racism is our job. They emphasize that "there is a clear need for social scientists to identify ethnic differences, to explain them . . . and to find ways to diminish their capacity to fuel conflict."

Instead of reaching toward this ambitious goal, researchers often narrow their focus to tease out minor distinctions within an already established intervention method. For example, let's recall the illustrative intervention earlier in this chapter that considered sending reminders to bike as a way of shifting the commuting behavior of people in Washington, DC. Researchers would be rewarded, in terms of academic attention and publishing opportunities, for designing an intervention (a "horse race") with multiple treatment arms that could tease out the impact of sending people reminders to bike that were on paper, sent via text, sent via email, in bold, in color, in black and white, fully in emojis, and so on. Behavioral interventions are often designed with multiple arms to answer these interesting, but small, questions while never naming the larger sociocultural issues. It's as if the higher order goals Ross and Nisbett laid out have been diminished.

In fact, the tools of behavioral science can play a role in exposing racist structures and illuminating the challenges that lay ahead. This is indeed our job, and when we fail to do that job, our research suffers. For example, when we tried to shift savings behavior at VITA sites, we asked, How can we get people to save for retirement or in savings bonds? But given structural forces that increase debt for BIPOC populations, this was the wrong question. We should have been asking how we could help manage that debt. Moreover, our research design should have attempted to capture and expose the size of the racialized debt gap between white and BIPOC VITA clients and identify the structural forces that have led to that gap. Designing research this way would have been more responsive to people's lives and ultimately may have had a better chance at achieving positive impacts.

In addition, when our interventions focus on individual-scale approaches to behavior change, we inadvertently look away from systemic issues. For example, an experiment designed to nudge consumers into saving a bit more money each month might be considered successful, but it also frames the problem as one of individual failures (even if we call them cognitive biases) and leaves the fundamental inequities resident in our financial systems intact, uncatalogued, and unquestioned.

The good news is that we can improve our research practices. Two seminal studies provide examples.

WHAT IS POSSIBLE

When examining the history of social science, there are several landmark examples of how a consideration of deeply entrenched structural problems could and should be considered in the design and implementation of policy. Here we examine two well-known examples: the "doll study" and the Robbers Cave experiments.

The Doll Study

In the 1930s and 1940s, Kenneth and Mamie Clark (both Black psychologists) conducted studies to explore how segregation impacted the psyche of young Black children. The children (between the ages of three and seven) were asked about their preferences between Black and white dolls, along with their perceptions of the dolls. Most children preferred the white doll and described it more favorably than the Black doll. When asked which doll was the "nice" one, for example, children overwhelmingly chose the white doll. Most Black children also chose the white doll when asked which one was most like them and became upset when it was suggested that they might be more like the Black doll.[11]

The results of this groundbreaking study were used in the *Brown v. Board of Education* Supreme Court case (citing the Clarks's research).[12] Specifically, it was noted that school segregation had a potential to create harm for Black children. The paper concluded that racism is a deeply rooted American institution and that a failure to desegregate schools would impact the development of white children as well.

This case provides a great example of an instance where an understanding of individual psychology was tied to broader system-level and institutional-level problems and their potential solutions. Even though this was a study with some very valid methodological issues (small sample size, no true control group), it attempted to examine decision-making with a conscious consideration of the underlying thread of racism in the United States. There have been several recreations of this experiment that found some improvement in Black children's attitudes but also found many of the same prejudices among white children.[13] Despite the many changes in American society, the heartbreaking findings persist.

Robbers Cave

Another famous social psychology study was a series of experiments examining conflict between groups, conducted by Muzafer Sherif (a Turkish American psychologist) and colleagues.[14] This work originated in the 1940s, shortly after the Clarks published their doll research. Boys at a summer camp in Robbers Cave State Park, Oklahoma, were divided into two groups, and the researchers observed how they created group norms. When introduced to each other (after some time to create group cohesion), conflict developed very quickly between the two groups and cohesion increased within the groups.

When the boys encountered a series of (shared and staged) challenges, the researchers found that focusing on shared goals created cohesion between the groups and increased positive perceptions. The study was the most famous demonstration of realistic group conflict theory, which hypothesized that positive relations between groups can only be restored after conflict when there are superordinate goals.

While tested in a manipulated environment, these findings were subsequently applied to real-world challenges, such as education and racial divides. Specifically, Sherif's insight led to the development of an educational approach called the "jigsaw classroom."

After the *Brown v. Board of Education* decision, schools across America were desegregated through the 1960s and 1970s. A Texas school district asked Elliot Aronson,[15] another social psychologist, to design interventions that might reduce conflict between racial groups in the newly desegregated schools. The Robbers Cave study directly influenced Aronson's jigsaw classroom design.

In this approach, a class or team is divided into groups that have been intentionally set up to be as diverse as possible, considering factors like gender, ethnicity, and cultural background. Within these groups, everyone is responsible for learning one key piece of information and teaching it to the rest of their group in the service of a shared superordinate goal. Aronson's intervention directly acknowledged and addressed the significant undercurrent of racism and stereotyping present in these newly desegregated classrooms. He then used insights from social psychology to address them, with impressive results.[16] Classrooms using the jigsaw classroom approach had decreased stereotyping and prejudice, along with improved test performance and measures of self-esteem.

These two examples will be incredibly instructive as we chart a way forward.

4 BEHAVIORAL SCIENCE IN ACTION: STANDARD TOOLS AND PRACTICES

> The cultural images and messages that affirm the assumed superiority of Whites and the assumed inferiority of people of color is like smog in the air. Sometimes it is so thick it is visible, other times it is less apparent, but always, day in and day out, we are breathing it in.
>
> —BEVERLY DANIEL TATUM

Before describing our proposed pathway forward, we use this chapter to examine the various steps that researchers and practitioners typically use to identify behavioral challenges and design for potential solutions. In chapter 5, we'll explore concrete actions to be taken in the service of antiracist behavioral design.

THE TRADITIONAL MODEL

The method of identifying behavioral challenges (often termed "behavioral diagnosis and design" or "behavioral mapping") is intended to take a comprehensive and objective approach to understanding the challenges in a decision context before designing potential solutions. Ideally, researchers take these steps to design approaches that are relevant, actionable, and testable for a specific challenge. The process is intended to increase the likelihood of an intervention's success by identifying problematic assumptions early on.

However, the process was not initially designed to uncover structural issues like racism. One of the earliest descriptions of the behavioral mapping process stated that "the first step to finding a solution is identifying the root of the problem." But the authors, and we as a field, have not really meant for this process to identify "root" causes. Instead, it was meant to identify individual-level, psychological barriers, as the paper makes clear in the next paragraph when it presents forgetfulness as a possible root problem.[1]

The typical process of designing and testing behavioral interventions includes the following steps:

1. *Defining the problem.* In this step, the team collaborates to decide on a primary objective. Typically, this is done without making any assumptions as to the root cause of the problem meant to be addressed. The definition of the problem should involve a clear behavioral element.
2. *Discovering or diagnosing the behavioral roadblocks to desired behavior* (where exactly in the process to intervene). This is an information gathering phase where the researchers attempt to learn about the cause of the behavioral problem (we often refer to these factors as behavioral "bottlenecks"). This can be done using all types of data, though behavioral scientists have traditionally relied disproportionately on observational and administrative data.
3. *Designing behaviorally informed interventions.* The insights gained in the previous step are now used to design the intervention meant to address the behavioral issue identified in step 1.
4. *Testing the impacts of those interventions.* Studies (often randomized controlled trials, RCTs) are used to measure the impact of the interventions.
5. *Sharing the results (and sometimes scaling the approach).* The findings are shared with relevant stakeholders, often published in an academic publication, and sometimes applied more widely as appropriate and feasible.

The behavioral design process borrows from the ideation design process and design thinking made popular by groups like IDEO, an international design and consulting firm and its nonprofit arm, IDEO.org. Often, insights uncovered at various steps may prompt a research team to revert to an earlier stage of the process. Recently, there have been efforts in the graphic and industrial design fields to update these processes, with the goal of engaging in inclusive design. The applied behavioral sciences have not gone through this evolution—yet.

THE UPDATED MODEL

In the pursuit of a better application of behavioral science, we're guided by two goals. First, we want to change the *direction* of behavioral design and behavioral science. Traditionally, applied behavioral science functions like a one-way street: bringing behavioral insights to NGOs and government agencies from academia. Mindy's first job title in the field really underscores this. As one of the first employees at ideas42, where formal titles were not yet the norm, her working title was "Roving Scholar." The idea was that she would roam around from NGO to government agency, dropping behavioral insights and designing interventions. However, at that time, the work did not actively engage the participants in developing theories and research methods.[2]

Instead of a one-way street where designs come from behavioral science to the community, we want to build a bridge where insights flow from behavioral science to the community *and* from the community to behavioral science. In this new flow, insights and designs evolve and become more nuanced and relevant to impacted communities. The NIH has been supporting work like this since 2005. For example, its Community-Based Participatory Research Program supports research in which scientists and communities collaboratively address health disparities, with research questions determined by the *community's* priorities, allowing impacted communities to take the lead in identifying research topics.[3]

Second, we must embed BIPOC perspectives on the social issues that impact them in systematic, concrete ways. It's a more ethical approach, and it makes our work more accurate, relevant, and impactful. It can also minimize harmful unintended consequences. While we seldom acknowledge it, our research has the potential to do harm when we leave out critical perspectives. So, inclusion is not a vague goal. It's an essential component of good applied behavioral science and should be ensured by budgets, staff recruitment, explicit research goals, and accountability systems. In research that impacts relevant communities, we need to track BIPOC inclusion like it's a dependent variable.

Below, we update the traditional behavioral design process by briefly describing the goal and process of each current step and then presenting our amendments to that step. Figure 4.1 shows our reimagined map of an

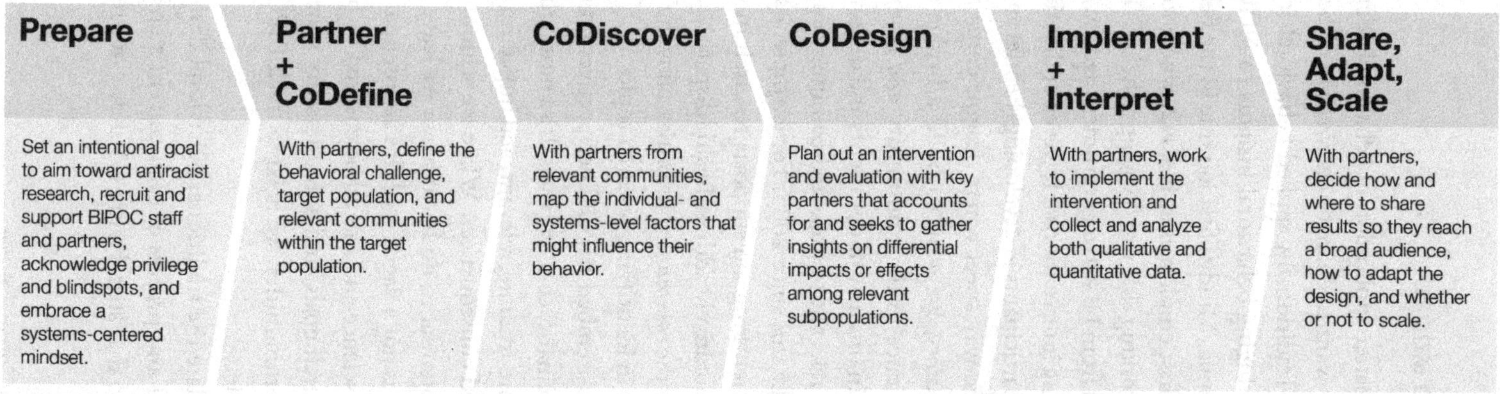

Prepare	Partner + CoDefine	CoDiscover	CoDesign	Implement + Interpret	Share, Adapt, Scale
Set an intentional goal to aim toward antiracist research, recruit and support BIPOC staff and partners, acknowledge privilege and blindspots, and embrace a systems-centered mindset.	With partners, define the behavioral challenge, target population, and relevant communities within the target population.	With partners from relevant communities, map the individual- and systems-level factors that might influence their behavior.	Plan out an intervention and evaluation with key partners that accounts for and seeks to gather insights on differential impacts or effects among relevant subpopulations.	With partners, work to implement the intervention and collect and analyze both qualitative and quantitative data.	With partners, decide how and where to share results so they reach a broad audience, how to adapt the design, and whether or not to scale.

Figure 4.1
An updated approach to behavioral intervention design.

antiracist behavioral intervention design process. In chapters 6–11, we'll dive into each step in detail.

NEW STEP: STEP 0: PREPARE (CHAPTER 6)

We add this step to reflect the reality that creating antiracist designs takes forethought and intention. Preparation to dive into antiracist work should happen well before the urgency and deadlines of an impending project.

Preparing your workplace means intentionally recruiting people of color as part of your team and as project partners and ensuring that budget, timelines, and publication and dissemination plans are created to facilitate equal and authentic contributions. This process might also include the team working to educate themselves on the context and circumstances experienced by the community with whom they will partner. A team without lived experience in some domain shouldn't assume that bringing additional teammates in who *do* have lived experience absolves them from doing their own work to prepare.

STEP 1: PARTNER AND CODEFINE (CHAPTER 7)

In this stage, partners identify the challenges or problems of interest within a specific program, government agency, or nonprofit. To be most effective, the problem definition should be clearly linked to a specific behavior. For example, a behavioral challenge could be defined as "how can we encourage more people to vote?" But specifics are critical, and so at this stage, teams try to narrow this down to something more specific like, "how can we encourage young people between eighteen and twenty-five in Florida to vote in national elections?" In addition, the research question should be posed in a way that doesn't presume (explicitly or implicitly) a specific solution. A specific population and sometimes subpopulation of interest is also identified at this point.

In our experience, this is often the most overlooked stage of the process. Applied behavioral science was born in academia and continues to carry with it many of academia's fingerprints—both positive and negative. Our research often reflects hypotheses born in the minds of academics in search of a field laboratory. So, the "definition stage" can become academics simply defining a problem in terms of their specific research interests, which often don't overlap with their lived experiences. Further upstream, the problem may have been defined (at least in part) to meet the requirements of available funding. Often, those funders also lack lived experience with topics that US behavioral interventions focus on, like poverty, school failure, and debt.

Mindy can recall a moment early in her career that underlined for her why lived experience matters so much in this early stage. She was in a meeting discussing possible challenges involved in taking up student loans. It was a new project, and the team was in the early stages of defining the challenge. Only researchers were present. There were about a dozen people brainstorming possible barriers students face when they first receive their student loan letters. Mindy suggested that it might be confusing to see so many types of loans in one letter. Blank stares and silence from colleagues. She pushed on, "you remember when you got your student loan letter for the first time? And it listed all your loans—Perkins, Stafford, maybe a grant, a small scholarship, work study eligibility . . . it's a lot to take in. Uh, right?" Awkward silence. She scanned the room: not a flicker of recognition. Mindy was the only person in the room who had personally received a student loan letter.

Our revised process aims to make this type of situation rare if not impossible by baking in partnership from the very beginning. We suggest immediately partnering with communities that have direct experience with an issue and working together to define the challenge, key actors, and the goal of a potential intervention. We describe this phase as *partner and codefine* to clarify how these processes can be more inclusive and do a better job of sharing power and project ownership.

STEP 2: CODISCOVER (CHAPTER 8)

After a specific behavioral challenge has been defined, the next step is to explore the often wide-ranging behavioral factors that might be inhibiting the desired behavior. Ideally, researchers use qualitative[4] and quantitative[5] (often administrative) data to better understand the decision context and identify the specific barriers at play. We update the name of this process to *codiscover* to emphasize that this step ought to be collaborative.

In theory, deep formative research should happen here; but in practice, time and budget constraints, privacy regulations, and a lack of qualitative skills keep this stage short and underused. In the US public domain, surveying individuals can be quite complicated due to regulations protecting American privacy (and reducing burden). There is also a lack of researchers with expertise in qualitative methods—behavioral scientists tend to rely on the quantitative approaches where we have more training. And researchers may approach this stage with deeply held assumptions about the nature of the behavioral challenge, which tends to lead to a confirmatory approach.

Our failure to acknowledge racist structures often shows up at this point. Traditionally, we start this stage by creating behavioral maps, which identify the forces in decision environments that move individuals toward or away from certain behaviors. These maps help researchers identify where an intervention might help encourage, or discourage, certain behaviors. There are many ways to create a behavioral map. In figure 4.2, we present one framework we find helpful.[6] We have completed the map with possible insights (simplified for the sake of this example) from a discovery phase focused on increasing biking in DC. These are not meant to be the "right" answers.

Working from left to right, this map first has a place to name the behavioral challenge, then the key actor (or population) that the project will focus on, then the factors that enable or constrain (act as barriers to) behavior change, and, finally, the strategy that the behavioral intervention will use to address the factors and change behavior. Importantly, this illustrative map only includes individual-level actors, and therefore the factors considered and the strategy ultimately designed are created as a response to only individual-level considerations.

Structural barriers like redlining and employment discrimination, while they may be acknowledged, rarely become the places where behavioral scientists ultimately focus their intervention design efforts. As mentioned earlier, BIPOC communities' decision landscapes feature different, heavier barriers (factors) that aren't easily nudged to the side. An updated codiscovery stage aims to rectify this.

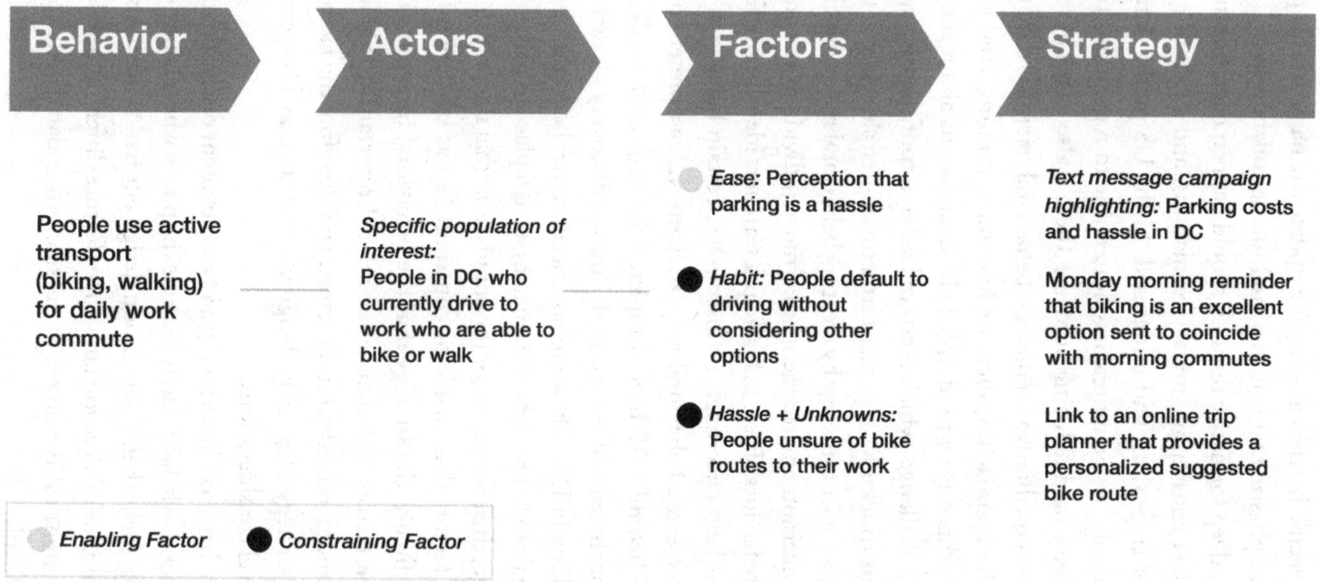

Behavior	Actors	Factors	Strategy
People use active transport (biking, walking) for daily work commute	*Specific population of interest:* People in DC who currently drive to work who are able to bike or walk	○ *Ease:* Perception that parking is a hassle	*Text message campaign highlighting:* Parking costs and hassle in DC
		● *Habit:* People default to driving without considering other options	Monday morning reminder that biking is an excellent option sent to coincide with morning commutes
		● *Hassle + Unknowns:* People unsure of bike routes to their work	Link to an online trip planner that provides a personalized suggested bike route

○ *Enabling Factor*   ● *Constraining Factor*

Figure 4.2
A standard behavioral map using an effort to encourage biking and walking as an illustrative example.

In our update, we propose a systems-based approach. Instead of disproportionately focusing on individual limitations (though those are certainly relevant), systems that drive oppression and racism should be directly acknowledged. This acknowledgment will increase the likelihood that the later work will be designed to name, quantify, and possibly disrupt systemic disparities.

An updated behavioral map template is shown in figure 4.3. The two key changes are 1) changing "actor" to "actors," with space dedicated to naming specific communities of interest to remind us that there are diverse communities within a population, and those communities will often have different constraints that should be considered; and 2) the addition of "systemic detractors" as a space to name systemic barriers that might be impacting people's ability to change their behavior.

As you can see from this revised illustrative map, we can now name specific communities, like BIPOC populations, and map out possible factors that might impact only (or especially) these communities. And we can consider both the individual factors, like fear of police violence, and systemic issues (or detractors), such as formal and informal police practices that have encouraged racial profiling. Other systemic issues could be added to this list, like a history of underinvestment in bike lanes in majority BIPOC neighborhoods.

Most behavioral interventions won't be able to devise a clever strategy to tackle these systemic issues, but they should be named and acknowledged. As we discuss in detail in later chapters, naming these challenges is valuable in at least four ways: it gives us context to understand why an intervention might have less impact in general and on some populations specifically, it allows us to identify and minimize unintended consequences, it provides critical data gathering opportunities, and it's an opportunity to pinpoint issues that must be acknowledged in the final paper or product. In the illustrative map above, you can see that naming police profiling as an underlying issue leads to a strategy not in the intervention design but in the data gathering design—specifically, to gather survey responses documenting to what extent fear of police violence acts as a barrier to biking for BIPOC communities.

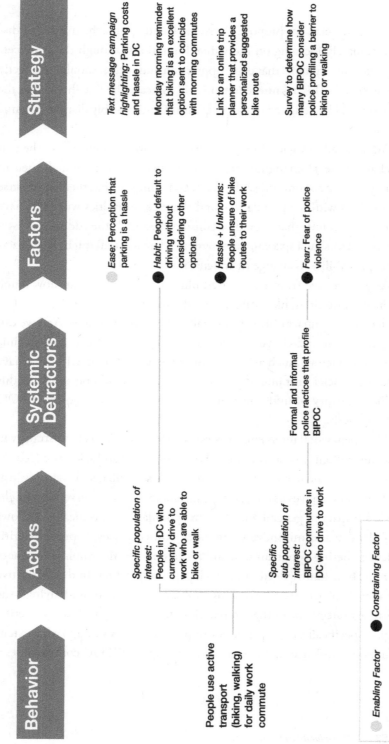

Figure 4.3
An updated behavioral map with structural considerations using an effort to encourage biking and walking as an illustrative example.

In this codiscover phase we work with partners to create maps like the one above to identify and then properly describe (via both quantitative and qualitative measures) the key actors and the unique barriers and opportunities that confront them at both an individual and systemic level.

STEP 3: CODESIGN (CHAPTER 9)

Some articulations of the traditional process discuss this stage only in terms of intervention design. In practice, the intervention and evaluation must be designed together because they inform each other. We therefore discuss both intervention and evaluation design at this stage.

Designing the intervention: Once the barriers have been identified, an intervention approach is designed. The goal is to design an intervention that decreases identified barriers or uses behavioral insights to make the target behavior easier to achieve. As discussed, usually the only barriers an intervention addresses are at the individual level or are cognitive/behavioral in nature. For example, the FAFSA intervention we described earlier focused on increasing college loan completion and identified hassle as a barrier. The intervention's design then aimed to decrease the hassle of form completion. But the intervention didn't identify the racial wealth gap as a barrier. In our update, we recognize that a behavioral intervention cannot reduce the barrier of America's racialized wealth gap. However, our intervention would be designed *in light of* the wealth gap and the history of predatory loans aimed at BIPOC. Therefore, as described earlier, our intervention might also include shortcuts that make weeding out predatory loans and institutions easier.

At this stage, we want to deepen our work with partners (who we've already involved in steps 0–2) to design an intervention that responds to realistic and critical barriers. Traditionally, this stage involves only behavioral scientists (and potentially funders). Our revised version includes relevant community members as both participants and decision makers.

Designing the evaluation: We should evaluate the impact of our interventions whenever possible to understand whether or not the approaches work at improving the desired outcomes. The evaluation might be nonexperimental, quasi-experimental, or an RCT[7] design, depending on the data, budget, and stakeholder interest. RCTs are considered the "gold standard." Because academics often design interventions with an eye toward publication, there's a focus on using RCTs that can be published in journals viewed as influential in academic circles.

Our updated description of this phase continues to prioritize RCTs but also recommends considering other methodologies (either as a substitute or as a complement to an RCT). Because BIPOC samples can be smaller than white samples, the BIPOC populations may be too small to reach statistical significance. Often, this results in RCT research omitting a thorough exploration of how the intervention impacted them. Making room for qualitative methods can ensure their voices and experiences are documented.

Whatever the experimental design of the evaluation, we want to collect and eventually disaggregate nuanced race and ethnicity data to help ensure that the evaluation can further antiracist goals. Too often, behavioral research fails to collect even basic demographic data.[8]

While evaluations are sometimes designed exclusively by researchers, we recommend that projected partners are part of the design process. We rename this step *codesign* to underline that this step should be participatory and collaborative.

STEP 4: IMPLEMENT AND INTERPRET (CHAPTER 10)

We rename this step for two reasons. First, aside from updating to reflect antiracist practices, calling this step "testing" fails to inadequately reflect what happens in practice. When an intervention launches in the field, many activities are taking place, not just the "testing." For example, researchers are collaborating with partners and running quality control on the intervention to be sure it's implemented with fidelity. Therefore, we add the term "implement."

Second, referring to this phase as testing infers that understanding the results from the "test" is a straightforward exercise in counting and comparing test version A to test version B. It's true that traditionally, all data is gathered and analyzed at this point. And often, that data is quantitative only and without nuanced demographic data so the analysis can be straightforward. But we add the term "interpret" to reflect that this stage should involve synthesizing information from different sources, including analyzing differential impacts on different communities.

For example, rigorous quantitative methods should be merged with qualitative methods that can add nuance and ensure feedback from diverse communities. A researcher trying to understand the relationship between tribal governments and the US government might have access to data that has been gathered over the years, which may help them understand high-level trends about outcomes such as public benefits usage. But an opportunity to conduct interviews with tribal leaders on their experiences would add color and nuance that could never be captured by the data alone. Even if the overall sample is small, interviews, focus groups, and surveys can help document the differential impacts on BIPOC communities. To ensure that the analysis furthers antiracist goals, we want our analysis to compare results by race, ethnicity, and other relevant variables (like gender and income), including looking at how multiple identities intersect and influence behaviors. (We discuss intersectionality in more detail in chapter 9.) At this point, results are written up and summarized. In the next phase, the researchers and partners decide how to package and share the findings.

STEP 5: SHARE, ADAPT, AND SCALE (CHAPTER 11)

After research is conducted, the results should be shared with all partners and others working on similar issues. This can be done via industry conferences, academic conferences, or smaller-scale events with relevant stakeholders. If an intervention has been deemed successful, the results can be shared more broadly and possibly be taken to scale. Efforts are made to share results with those who can replicate the study on a larger scale. However, behavioral science teams usually fail to circle back to the communities most directly impacted by their findings, and instead focus on higher-level partners (such as policymakers, funders, or other powerful gatekeepers).

Traditionally, only the behavioral scientists receive authorship on academic papers, but this could be shared with stakeholders and partners.

Academic conferences are often prioritized for sharing findings, but efforts should be made to present research at inclusive events that involve community members and recognize their contributions.

For example, when Mindy and Crystal conducted their research at free tax preparation sites in Philadelphia, they should have prioritized returning to share their findings with the staff, volunteer, and client community. This might have helped provide important context to what worked and what didn't work, improving the likelihood of success in any future research (or influencing whether the tax sites changed any of their practices).

We rename this *share, adapt, and scale* to reflect that this step should involve sharing results and occasionally scaling success, but will most often involve iterating and adapting. Adapting is a key but overlooked step that requires humility and flexibility. Teams must be willing to recognize that initial ideas may not be successful. In fact, when designs don't work, it's not failure—it's the scientific method. Teams must be flexible enough to quickly identify what didn't work, lean into what did, and try again. Going further, research teams should attempt to how any identify unintended effects (especially downstream effects) might snowball when the intervention is scaled.

While the traditional behavioral intervention design process has done an adequate job of serving applied behavioral science, there are critical shortcomings to the way this approach is typically practiced. In this section, we have highlighted some of these gaps, and in subsequent chapters, we will provide tools and strategies to address them in more detail.

5 A VISION OF SUCCESS

> Historically, pandemics have forced humans to break with the past and imagine their world anew. This one is no different. It is a portal, a gateway between one world and the next. We can choose to walk through it, dragging the carcasses of our prejudice and hatred, our avarice, our data banks and dead ideas, our dead rivers and smoky skies behind us. Or we can walk through lightly, with little luggage, ready to imagine another world. And ready to fight for it.
>
> —ARUNDHATI ROY

Many years ago, Mindy worked with Bank on DC, an organization with the mission of opening ten thousand bank accounts for unbanked households in the region. By teaming up with the Summer Youth Employment Program (SYEP), which offers summer jobs to fourteen- to twenty-one-year-olds, Bank on DC was hoping to bring financial education and the opportunity to open bank accounts to nearly nine thousand young DC residents.

In prior years, SYEP participants received their earnings on a prepaid card, which seemed like a neutral decision. However, making prepaid cards the "default" made it less likely that participants would open a bank account. Mindy proposed a new system in which participants could sign up for direct deposit on the same online system they used to sign up for SYEP. Payment via prepaid card would only be presented as an option if they rejected the bank account option.

The administering agency didn't like this design. It made them uncomfortable. They said they didn't want to influence people's choices. But because people are influenced by subtle aspects of their environment, it's nearly impossible to create a truly neutral choice set. In fact, by simply defaulting everyone into prepaid cards, as the agency did the year prior, they were acting "paternalistically" and steering choices in a specific (and effective!) way. That year, 100 percent of SYEP participants were paid via prepaid cards, and nobody took advantage of direct deposit or automatic savings.

AN ANTIRACIST APPROACH TO APPLIED BEHAVIORAL SCIENCE

This story underlines, as discussed early in this book, that there is no neutrality when it comes to designing policies and programs. When we design interventions, we're either reinforcing or resisting the status quo—including existing racist structures.

We'll repeat Kendi's important statement on the fallacy of race neutrality here: "Every policy in every institution in every community in every nation is producing or sustaining either racial inequity or equity between racial groups."

Borrowing from Kendi, we define *a racist policy* as any measure that produces or sustains racial inequity between racial groups and an *antiracist policy* as any measure that produces or sustains racial equity between racial groups.

Building on these definitions, "racist" behavioral science application includes any intervention that *directly or indirectly* produces or sustains racial inequity between racial groups. Antiracist application of behavioral science includes any intervention designed to identify or quantify racial inequities, or to produce or sustain racial equity between racial groups.

We recognize that this may seem like an ambitious definition of what applied behavioral science can and should do. To clarify, we don't think that every behavioral intervention should aim to take down racist practices. But we do believe that behavioral scientists have an opportunity and a responsibility to play a role in pushing toward justice. Consider Drs. Kenneth and Mamie Clark who coauthored the doll study. They didn't veer from their core role as psychologists seeking to understand how children understood themselves and the world around them. But they used their tools to shine a light on racism's impact on children.

Considering racism in our research processes can expose and quantify the magnitude of racist practices, allowing us to minimize intervention side effects. This practice can even begin to challenge, if not dismantle, race-based barriers in our intervention designs. Outcomes of successful antiracist behavioral design include increased overall impact, increased access to the field, a limitation of negative unintended consequences, and an awareness of racial differences in outcomes (even if they can't be addressed).

When we fail to play our role, we become part of the problem. If behavioral interventions are simply embedded into racist policies and practices, our approaches and nudges will just reinforce existing unjust systems, and the outcomes of our interventions may result in the design, implementation, and scaling of racist designs and policies.

While behavioral science alone may not be able to dismantle America's racist superstructures, there are still steps we can take to avoid blindly affirming them. Let's consider how this might work.

Recall two studies we introduced in chapters 1 and 2: text messages to increase bike use in Washington, DC, and simplification to increase FAFSA completion and college-going. How would an antiracist revise and update these studies?

In our illustrative case study on text messages, attempts to increase the use of a city's bike share system didn't challenge underlying transportation barriers. A revised approach could begin with the researchers acknowledging that Washington, DC is a diverse city with a majority Black and Latino population (the most recent census revealed that Black and Latino residents make up 56.7 percent of the city's total population).[1] Like many large cities in America, it also has a violent history of racial segregation. Given this racist history, researchers might adjust their research design by adding extra time and budget to engage in interviews and conduct racially diverse focus groups (in addition to executing a standard literature review). Recalling the updated behavioral map we presented in chapter 3, this formative research would uncover key actors and the individual- and systems-level barriers they face. The goal of this work would be to create testable hypotheses about the factors that might explain why some people have not yet taken up the city's bike share system.

In addition, a revised intervention could expose and estimate the magnitude of the problem by intentionally collecting a diverse sample (with respect to race and gender) and documenting the differential use of bikes/scooters and barriers faced by BIPOC communities, including racial profiling. Further, the evaluation design could include postintervention focus groups to understand why some communities did not change their behavior. This approach would help to identify the issue, understand the magnitude of the challenge, and widely share those results. Perhaps the intervention is the same: text messages are sent telling people where to find the nearest bike and where to find protected bike lanes in their neighborhood. The difference is that now the results of the study could raise a potent issue: that a number of BIPOC residents worry about police violence and profiling on their daily commute, and this impacts their lives.

The resulting study could also include an informative map of where protected bike lanes exist in the city so that city officials can rectify any imbalance, and transportation justice activists can call them to task if they do not. Our new intervention uses the standard behavioral science tools, but now those tools do double duty, quantifying the systemic barriers the city's large BIPOC population faces. Using our definition, this has become an antiracist application of behavioral science because it has been designed to identify and quantify racial inequities. By giving local activists data they need, it may also increase accountability and produce increased racial equity.

Let's also revisit the federal student aid (FAFSA) completion study. Recall that various interventions were designed to help tax filers with low incomes apply for financial aid while they were getting help preparing their taxes. Because tax sites already had significant financial information, they were able to prepopulate much of the FAFSA form, making it easier to complete.

The interventions were largely successful in increasing FAFSA completion and college attendance, which means these well-meaning studies likely increased debt among BIPOC families. Given research on race and college debt, it's likely (though not yet documented) that these studies may have inadvertently increased the number of BIPOC students with debt that they're unable to pay off. The studies did not disaggregate results by race and ethnicity or follow subjects after school enrollment so it is hard to know the impact on BIPOC borrowers.

With the understanding that loan repayment and debt look different for BIPOC borrowers, a future study would aim beyond immediate FAFSA completion to postsecondary school completion with manageable debt. It would intentionally collect data by race and ethnicity.

The work would begin much earlier at the partnership and codefine stage. Instead of only partnering with tax sites, researchers would forge partnerships with financial empowerment NGOs and relevant postsecondary schools. To reveal potential pitfalls in loan repayment and quantify possible racialized wealth gaps, formative research would explore financial barriers, income goals, and family debt obligations across race, ethnicity, and income levels.

The intervention would then be designed to tackle two key challenges: (1) helping tax filers, especially BIPOC and low-income students, identify low-risk loans and high-quality schools with strong graduation rates; and (2) supporting them through postsecondary school completion and successful loan repayment. In partnership with financial empowerment NGOs, the intervention would still lean into the idea of simplification by developing accessible tools to screen out schools with low graduation rates and match students with scholarships. With prepopulated tax data, tools would automatically estimate post-graduation debt burdens compared to projected income, providing clear financial forecasts.

Next, the design would aim to help those who complete the FAFSA finish postsecondary school with successful loan repayment. (Yes, this is a multiyear study, which is challenging to implement, but this is our fan fiction, so we want to paint a picture of what is possible, even if it's not easy.) In partnership with select colleges, researchers could connect students with peers from similar backgrounds, providing mentorship, information on job opportunities, and support.

Finally, the evaluation would look beyond initial FAFSA completion and seek to understand if the intervention resulted in optimal aid packages from schools with high graduation rates, college completion, and loan repayment success. By disaggregating the outcome data by race, ethnicity, and income, the evaluation would quantify any gaps by race and ethnicity. Correlating initial wealth gaps with loan repayment success could further illuminate systemic barriers.

This intervention would not resolve racialized wealth gaps, but it would identify, quantify and respond to them.

So how do we go about transforming these "fan fiction" studies into best, and then common, practice? As behavioral scientists, we advise a feasible approach that makes behavior change easy, which we lay out in the following chapters.

II THE ROADMAP TO CHANGE

Crystal vividly remembers giving a talk about her work with the Office of Evaluation Sciences (OES) to her faculty and student colleagues at the University of Washington in 2016. Toward the end of the session, a friend asked how the OES was engaging in issues of equity.

Crystal was immediately stumped and then incredibly embarrassed. She gave the typical party line about the limitations of not having access to the appropriate "samples" to engage in what she would now describe as antiracist methodologies. At the time, being embedded in that work felt like such an enormous opportunity that any pushback against it raised her anxiety about being seen as too disruptive in a (largely white) field she cared deeply about. In retrospect, she also felt largely beholden to this community. That moment was a wake-up call to start asking harder questions and insisting that colleagues and partners do the same. For far too long, we have remained silent and complicit in perpetuating problems that lie at the core of our work.

As good behavioral scientists, we believe that part of the answer is making it easy to both use new tools and to use old tools differently. In the next section, we'll take a deep dive into our reimagined path, starting with our new and essential first step: prepare your workplace.

6 PREPARE YOUR WORKPLACE

> History never really says goodbye. History says, "See you later."
> —EDUARDO GALEANO

This step isn't mentioned in any applied behavioral science frameworks we know of, probably because there's an assumption that people who engage in behavioral science projects are already prepared with a classic behavioral science education, experience in the field, and coursework in social science methods and statistics. Cultural literacy, a background in systems-level analysis, race theory, and lived experience with the social issues we tackle is not (in our experience) ever required.

This is an oversight. Understanding systemic racism is not a given in American life. In fact, the opposite is true: a recent study found that most white (70 percent), Asian (65 percent), and Hispanic (63 percent) adults believe that racism by individuals is a bigger issue than institutional racism against Black people.[1] Only 43 percent of Black Americans thought the same.

Gaps in adult knowledge are unsurprising given what most American high schoolers are taught. As the comedian and author Trevor Noah joked, "In America, the history of racism is taught like this: 'There was slavery and then there was Jim Crow and then there was Martin Luther King Jr. and now it's done.'" He has a point. According to a 2018 study by the Southern Poverty Law Center, only 8 percent of American high school seniors could identify slavery as the central cause of the Civil War.[2] The study also found that many students had a limited understanding of the historical and ongoing impacts of racism, including redlining, mass incarceration, and police brutality.

Scholars and activists such as Angela Davis (a rare exemplar of both) have argued that systems and structures within the United States were key to understanding the impacts of issues such as mass incarceration and education disparities. She fought for coordinated engagement of seemingly distinct but interconnected communities (Black, Indigenous, incarcerated, those living in poverty) to address deeply rooted issues like incarceration, poverty, and domestic violence. She recognized that these communities were bound together by similar systems of control. Focusing on individual-level barriers and behaviors conceals the larger interconnected systems of oppression. Not surprisingly, given that she deeply understood the power of intersecting marginalized identities, Davis was also a pioneer in the fight for gender and gay rights.

However, the behavioral science community at large is often ignorant of these important perspectives and the history behind them. As a result, we dive into intervention design around social struggles like poverty, unemployment, and debt unprepared to acknowledge, explore, and address structural racism and its connection to larger systems of oppression. Instead, we discuss race in the narrow way we've been trained to: as a demographic characteristic rather than a determinative factor lying (unacknowledged) beneath our interventions.

We've added this first step, "prepare your workplace," to challenge the assumption that a traditional behavioral science education is sufficient preparation. Instead, we broaden the definition of being "prepared" to include being prepared to take an antiracist approach to our work. Several strategies are described below.

"IMPORTANT ENOUGH THAT YOU HAVE TO RISK IT ALL"

The psychologists Steven Roberts and Michael Rizzo coined the term "proactive antiracism"[3] to describe a mindset where individuals and groups attempt to challenge and avoid racism before it occurs. For behavioral research teams, this means setting an intentional goal to understand the issue being studied from a BIPOC perspective and, more ambitiously, to design antiracist interventions. Recall that we define antiracist practices as those designed to *identify or quantify racial inequities or to produce or sustain racial equity between racial groups*. How does this work in practice?

Let's look at the story of Ana Patricia Muñoz, a determined economist who had been working for a decade at the Federal Reserve Bank of Boston. Muñoz cared about racial equity, and when she heard that researchers in other cities were looking at racial wealth gaps, she knew she wanted to do the same in Boston. However, her initial proposal was met with reluctance from her bosses. "I don't know if fear is the word, but apprehension of what [could] happen and, 'Is it really the Fed's role to do this?'" Muñoz told the radio station, WBUR. But she persisted, convinced that the research aligned with the Fed's mission. "This [was] important enough that you have to risk it all to do it," she said.[4] She convinced her colleagues in Boston and collaborated with regional Federal Reserve Banks and notable researchers like William Darity Jr. and Darrick Hamilton.

Muñoz's persistence paid off. The resulting findings were notable for the stark disparities they uncovered: in 2014, the median white household had a net worth $247,500. The median nonimmigrant Black household: $8.[5] The data galvanized local activists, turning the research into a central pillar for tackling racial wealth inequalities.

It was even featured on the *Daily Show*, in a scene where a reporter from the *Boston Globe* explains the findings to Roy Wood Jr., the hilarious *Daily Show* correspondent. "Eight . . . like [Black families in Boston have] eight thousand dollars?" he asks, confused. "No. Just eight," the reporter explains. Wood Jr. goes on, "Eight dollars? That's not even a grande soy latte," he says as he sips a latte. "That's not even enough for a foot long," he says as he takes a bite of a sub. "That's not even enough to buy twelve—" he takes a doughnut from a box "—eleven doughnuts!" The reporter explains that the disparity is "one example of what structural racism looks like." Wood Jr. says through bites of his doughnut and sub, "I'm sorry . . . I eat when I'm sad about social inequality." The clip has been viewed more than ten million times.

Establishing an intention and persevering even in the face of institutional resistance, as Muñoz did, can sow the seeds for valuable insights that resonate broadly and serve as a rallying point for justice-oriented initiatives.

Approaching research with this mindset in the face of resistance can feel uncomfortable. It requires an implicit acknowledgment that we don't have all the answers, may not even know the right questions to ask, and probably need to lean on new, less familiar methodologies and partners. In the example above, Muñoz reached out to Black economists William Darity Jr. and Darrick Hamilton who had led similar research efforts. Acknowledging and pushing through that discomfort, instead of stopping there, might be the seed to building better behavioral science. As the great bell hooks has written, "true resistance begins with people confronting pain . . . and wanting to do something to change it."[6]

RECRUIT AND SUPPORT BIPOC STAFF AND PARTNERS

Representation influences what gets studied and how. Research by Steven O. Roberts and colleagues looked at twenty-six thousand psychology papers from 1974 to 2018 and found that only 5 percent discussed race. When journal editors were white, the proportion of articles focused on race dropped to less than 4 percent, but with BIPOC editors it tripled. Their research also found that when white researchers do conduct psychological studies that address race, they tend to use primarily white samples (and smaller proportions of BIPOC participants) compared to samples that BIPOC scholars compile.[7] So if we eventually want research that explores the lives and barriers of BIPOC communities, we need more BIPOC researchers and partners.

To do this well, we must first examine what specific expertise and perspectives are needed. It's a reflection of both how uncomfortable we are when talking about race and how racial groups have been vilified that many people can't bring themselves to even name specific races, as if naming a race makes you racist. A perfect fictional example comes from the television show *The Office* when Michael Scott, the ham-handed boss, is leading a diversity training and says to Oscar, the accountant who is Mexican American, "lemme ask you . . . is there a term besides Mexican that you prefer? Something . . . less offensive?"

Discomfort talking about race doesn't just live in Michael Scott's fictional office; it's alive in all offices. We both experienced this firsthand when a well-meaning colleague asked us how to phrase a position description for a behavioral science organization that was looking to hire BIPOC researchers. They phrased the ad as "looking for diverse perspectives," which they knew was not specific enough. They just felt uncomfortable saying "Black and Latino."

Recruiting, training, and supporting BIPOC staff and partners requires funding, accountability, and coordination. Institutions should earmark funds to recruit talent and invest in antiracist research. They should also hold themselves accountable by tracking the diversity of their workforce and research topics, and they should specifically make efforts to ensure BIPOC staff are being supported. This includes ensuring BIPOC staff are not treated as "token" hires but are intentionally given promotable work to give them the best chance to succeed.

A helpful example of how to execute these ideas in the real world comes from the NIH who, in 2021, publicly made a commitment to address structural racism in biomedical research. First, they made their intention crystal clear: "The time for NIH to take an active stance against structural racism is long overdue. NIH can no longer look the other way."[8] Then, they put dollars into this commitment by creating multiple grants earmarked for BIPOC researchers and the study of structural racism, including setting aside up to $30 million to fund research specifically focused on understanding and addressing the impact of structural racism and discrimination on the health of BIPOC Americans. The NIH also looked inward at racism's impact on biomedical research and allocated funds to understand and address the impact of structural racism and discrimination on career progression in their field.

The NIH held themselves accountable by first naming and acknowledging the persistent disparities in success rates for grants supporting Black scientists. They then created a process to gather and make public demographic data about their research workforce. In 2021, the Office of Extramural Research at NIH released a report that for the first time publicly stating grantee demographics by race/ethnicity.[9]

ACKNOWLEDGE YOUR PRIVILEGE AND LIMITATIONS

As the writer Ijeoma Oluo has argued, "when we identify where our privilege intersects with somebody else's oppression, we'll find our opportunities to make real change."[10] Recognizing the advantages and opportunities that come with being part of a dominant group can help research teams see their gaps and limitations. Research teams may not have the same cultural knowledge or lived experiences as the communities they're studying and therefore will have to make an intentional effort to partner and learn from those who do.

With the World Resources Institute (WRI), Mindy was working on a project to identify barriers to active transport (swapping car use for biking, walking, and other physical endeavors) in US cities. Consulting the literature and her own (privileged) experiences, safety and hassle appeared to be the "barrier" around which to design an intervention. Living in Washington, DC, Mindy biked around the city with her two young children, often in fear for their safety (and with a lot of biking on sidewalks, to the annoyance of many pedestrians). There were "bike lanes," but they were in no way protected. The "bike lanes" were really just smears of white paint. From her lived experience, increasing the real and perceived sense of road safety felt like the problem to solve.

WRI's mobility team had made capturing BIPOC experiences an explicit goal, and so, digging deeper into the literature (conducted outside of traditional academic journals), Mindy found a sliver of research that the researcher Charles Brown conducted specifically with people who identified as Black, Latino, or mixed race. Brown's research suggested that "arrested mobility" issues like fear of police profiling and police violence that impact BIPOC communities, especially men, may also play an important role in influencing whether people bike or not.[11]

Mindy's privilege of moving through the world looking like a white woman impacted her approach to the behavioral challenge. If she had designed an intervention based on that alone, the resulting intervention would have failed to name and confront police profiling and redlining as fundamental barriers to change.

Actively identifying areas of privilege among research team members helps uncover gaps and blind spots. This awareness enables the team to mitigate biases resulting from their privilege, like intentionally seeking out research from BIPOC researchers to understand different experiences.

EDUCATE YOURSELF AND YOUR TEAM

Most Americans, especially white Americans, don't arrive to work with a background in BIPOC history, critical race theory, or systems-centered framework and language. In fact, research has shown that rather than becoming more fluent in racism, as white children age, they are less able to acknowledge racial differences.[12] Not surprisingly, a recent Pew Research Center survey found that half of white Americans rarely or *never* talk about race relations with family and friends. (In comparison, 36 percent of Black Americans say they rarely or never talk about race).[13]

To begin to account for this deficit, teams should make an effort to provide training, coursework, and book clubs that allow staff to become more informed on these topics.[14] To that end, beginning with this chapter and continuing to chapter 11, we provide an antiracist checklist at the end of each chapter for each step of our updated process. At the end of the book, we also offer additional resources as a starting point. The leadership of research teams should determine what is needed based on where the team's blind spots lie.

It's worth noting that all training is not equal, and many are not effective. Time, effort, and intention should be spent bringing in high-quality, culturally relevant support. As has been documented, prejudice reduction strategies are often ineffective.[15] Even strategies that do seem effective have relatively modest effects. Training must be one component of a multifaceted strategy—not a substitute for the other actions we discuss here.

A checklist of good antiracist practices at this stage might include the following:

- Acknowledging the privileges within a team and areas where the current team lacks lived experience, and then using the suggestions below to make a plan to mitigate the blind spots that could arise from these gaps

- Reaching out to BIPOC behavioral science students as paid interns with the goal of attracting and retaining young talent in order to create a pipeline of talented BIPOC researchers (these young scholars ought to be paid for their work)
- Intentionally recruiting BIPOC staff and partners
- Creating project timelines and budgets that are generous enough to allow for thoughtful recruitment and hiring processes, staff trainings, and authentic codesign efforts
- Fostering partnerships with schools and communities that train BIPOC scholars
- Providing high-quality trainings, book clubs, and/or speakers to give research teams a background in BIPOC history, critical race theory, and systems-centered frameworks

7 PARTNER AND CODEFINE

They wanted our bodies in the room, but not our voices.
—JODI-ANN BUREY

Many years ago, Mindy sat in a small conference room with a group of education policy experts discussing how to help low-income, largely Black and Brown families sign their children up for small (presumably, better) charter schools rather than sending their kids to the local, lower-achieving public school.

This team didn't name the moment, but they were actively engaged in the *define* stage of a behavioral intervention design process. As discussed, the goal of this stage is to narrow the target behavior to the most specific and measurable framing possible, including defining the desired outcome and target population as specifically as possible. It's at this stage that a challenge defined too broadly as "how can we help people who are unbanked to open a bank account" becomes "how can we help *people using VITA sites in Detroit* without bank accounts to *open and use* accounts to save over a year." This hypothetical savings behavioral challenge is uncomplicated.

But reality often requires more nuance. Let's return to the conversation with Mindy's education policy colleagues.

As the meeting unfolded, what nagged at Mindy was the thought that she and her colleagues were misdefining the challenge. She remembered an old story. Her father, Victor, was a gifted student, and a teacher urged him to apply to Bronx Science, arguably the best public magnet school in New

York City. Her grandparents moved to the South Bronx from a small village in Puerto Rico and knew nothing about magnet schools. Despite his eventual acceptance into Bronx Science, Mindy's grandmother brushed off the suggestion and sent him to the local high school, the School of Machine and Metal Trade, with his older brother, Felix. According to the way Mindy's colleagues framed this very situation, her grandparents were misguided and needed to be persuaded to send Victor to the "better" school.

But it turned out the School of Machine and Metal Trade was a good choice, even if it was objectively not as high performing as Bronx Science. It was preparing students for jobs as metal workers, not for PhDs in engineering (which is where his education would take him eventually). But Mindy's dad felt comfortable there, and it gave him hands-on experience in building and constructing (tools he would later use in more abstract ways as a civil engineer). Moreover, as Mindy's grandmother rightly predicted, it allowed her uncle Felix, Victor's older brother, to be close to and protect Victor (who was not in any way "tough") from the violence of the South Bronx.

While not straightforward, a more thoughtfully defined behavioral challenge in this case might have been "how can we help local families identify the optimal school for their children?" We have both worked on several global health behavioral challenges where funders have defined the challenge as local community members not seeking various types of health care. But when we dove into the situation and spoke to the community, we found that people are sometimes making a rational choice to avoid low-quality, high-cost health care that tends to make them sicker and poorer.

So how do we move from an overly simplistic and problematic definition stage to one more realistic and relevant? Below we list four strategies to consider.

FORGE AUTHENTIC PARTNERSHIPS WITH RACIALLY AND ETHNICALLY DIVERSE GROUPS

When your team doesn't have lived experience in the domain/decision context, invite in partners who can help. It's important to do this early rather than starting a project and then inviting partners later, after the design is already cooked.

One specific strategy is to forge academic collaborations between predominantly white institutions (PWIs), where research resources tend to be higher, and historically Black colleges and universities (HBCUs), Hispanic-serving institutions (HSIs), and tribal colleges and universities (TCUs), where there are more BIPOC scholars.

It's worth pausing here to name that new partnerships aren't easy for white or BIPOC folks. Research by social psychologists Jennifer Richeson and Nicole Shelton has shown that interracial interactions leave people feeling drained both cognitively and emotionally. This is especially true for people of color. The additional emotional and cognitive load involved is likely a part of why interracial partnerships can be so difficult.[1]

Therefore, at this codefine stage, it's not enough to simply have white partners hold shared goals and values about the work (most of the time, they do!)—they must also understand and respect their BIPOC colleagues' additional emotional challenges, sometimes referred to as the "invisible labor" of being a person of color navigating white workplaces.

In the TV series *Insecure*, the writer and star Issa Rae makes the invisible labor of the main character, Issa, visible in her attempts to navigate her workplace, the fictional nonprofit, We Got Y'all (the name perfectly capturing the white savior complex of many well-meaning nonprofits).

Issa is the only Black person on staff, and as she describes it, "I've been here five years and they think I'm the token with the answers." Her white colleagues awkwardly ask her to explain everything from big questions (Issa's boss: "What would James Baldwin say is most beneficial to people of color?") to slang used by the kids in the tutoring program ("let's just ask Issa . . . what does 'on fleek' mean?") to their confusion about her wearing sunscreen during a field trip to the beach because, as her white colleague whispers to another white coworker, "I didn't think they'd even need any."

Rae has said that she wanted to show "that there's always layers to what's happening in any of our social interactions" and that she is often "quoting [sociologist and author W. E. B.] Dubois's concept of double consciousness, as in how we are always aware of how we're perceived."[2] As Du Bois defined it, double consciousness is the "sense of always looking at one's self through the eyes of others, of measuring one's soul by the tape of a world that looks on in amused contempt and pity."[3]

Given the extra work of navigating questions from white colleagues and work spaces that too often weren't built for BIPOC staff, Richeson and Shelton's findings about the emotional and cognitive load of interracial interactions are unsurprising. It's helpful for behavioral science teams to keep this in mind as they forge interracial partnerships. These challenges should not deter us from doing this work but should instead encourage teams to dedicate time to building real partnerships and friendships, and to offer grace in understanding that all parties may be working through discomfort.

FUNDRAISE HAND-IN-HAND WITH PARTNERS

Community partnerships with BIPOC organizations can increase trust and participation in research studies. To create deep and effective partnerships, BIPOC scholars and organizations should be invited to collaborate early in the funding proposal stage. Given that research often relies on grants, involving BIPOC partners as coapplicants who receive early funding support is essential. There's a common misconception among researchers that local groups are happy to be part of the process and have "their voices heard." However, everyone's time should be valued equally. Down the line, if a paper or article will be produced, that is valuable collateral, and community members who are part of the design or execution process should be offered coauthorship.

DEFINE THE "WHAT" AND THE "WHO" WITH PARTNERS AND WITH CONSIDERATION OF RACIST STRUCTURES

Traditionally, the individual with the power (policymaker, researcher, service provider, funder) frames the problem, which often leads to researchers making (typically unspoken and implicit) assumptions as to the nature of the appropriate solution or intervention. Instead, these stakeholders should reach out to relevant communities early to benefit from their perspective and understand whether the relevant community views the behavioral "problem" as a problem.

Additionally, research teams should discuss target populations and subpopulations with relevant partners to consider subgroups beyond the usual socioeconomic status. When relevant, it may help to consider nuances like colorism. For example, if studying issues that intersect with the police in any way, we know people with darker skin (whether African American, Latino, or mixed) are more likely to be arrested than those with similar racial backgrounds but with lighter skin.[4] Acknowledging this when thinking about a target population will make the subsequent research more impactful and exact. Imagine an intervention focused on decreasing repeat offenses. Research that has captured skin color in addition to the usual demographic variables might be able to shine a light on prejudiced treatment of darker skin participants.

DEFINE THE CHALLENGE IN LIGHT OF SYSTEMS-LEVEL BARRIERS

We need to move from a focus on individuals to systems-centered language and frameworks. Researchers often discusses risk factors attributed to a racial and ethnic group itself rather than to the conditions that members of this group have disproportionately experienced. In contrast, systems-centered language includes a discussion of the current policies and historical roots that maintain inequities.

For example, rather than noting that "BIPOC communities are more likely to experience poverty," our articulation of the challenge should be framed as "the systemic racism present in the economy and housing market leads to higher rates of poverty among BIPOC communities." This framing recognizes the root causes of disparities and highlights the need for systemic change.

Using systems-centered frameworks will help research teams identify the entrenched structural challenge the target population faces, rather than focusing on the actors who are caught in those structures. This approach shifts the focus from "blaming" individuals to examining and challenging the larger systemic forces at play. The "systemic detractors" section of the updated behavioral map presented in chapter 3 aims to help research teams take a systems-centered approach.

For example, without a systems-centered framework, a behavioral challenge might be defined as "how can we increase BIPOC students' motivation so they perform better academically?" With a systems-centered framework, the behavioral challenge might be redefined as "how can we help close the persistent opportunity gap between Black and white students given structural barriers like unequal funding, racial bias in teacher expectations, and limited access to quality educational resources?" The revised behavioral challenge identifies systemic issues and promotes systemic change.[5]

Racial equity tools can be useful at this stage. These are guides meant to help teams consciously integrate considerations of race and racism into their decision-making processes. They focus on not only the end result but also the process. In the codefine stage, they can help ensure that the team is ultimately landing on a problem that is aware of racial inequities. In too many cases, a problem is defined without even considering racial disparities, which might lead to inadvertently making those disparities worse. We suggest looking at tools such as the Government Alliance on Race and Equity's (GARE) Racial Equity Toolkit.[6] We include more resources at the end of the book.

A checklist of good antiracist practices at this stage might include the following:

- Creating ongoing partnerships with BIPOC community groups and postsecondary schools that can be involved in projects from the earliest conceptual, proposal writing, and design stages.
- Writing research proposals that budget for equal contributions from community partners (and compensating community partners for their time and effort). Proposals regularly compensate academic consultants and advisors; the same must be done for community members who lend their own expertise.
- Creating timelines that include plenty of time for partnership recruitment and relationship building.
- Using systems-centered language and frameworks when defining and describing the behavioral challenge and barriers.

8 CODISCOVER

> I wade through summer ghosts
> betrayed by vision
> hers and my own
> becoming dragonfish to survive
> the horrors we are living
> with tortured lungs
> adapting to breathe blood.
>
> —AUDRE LORDE

At this point, the table has been set, and it's time to dive into codiscovery. We use the term *discovery* to reframe the process as being open, formative, and iterative.[1]

The goal in this step is to unpack the various individual- and systems-level barriers (and potential opportunities) involved in changing the behavior described in the codefine phase. But too often, we approach this stage with preconceived notions. Instead, fully engaging in a formative codiscover stage provides valuable insights into the lived complexities and barriers that might make behavior change difficult. Using qualitative research methods is one important way we can gather formative insights.

In her work on the BIAS project, Crystal discovered some incredibly enlightening small focus groups conducted before the intervention design. The project's goal was to improve the rate at which parents who were incarcerated and did not have custody of their children applied for modifications to their child support orders. Without these modifications, parents would accrue significant debt, causing difficulties for everyone involved. Through focus groups with parents who had been recently released from prison, the team gained a deeper understanding of this confusing and overwhelming process. Crystal and her colleagues realized that some of their assumptions were inaccurate. They did not have a clear grasp on many of the details that informed the ultimate intervention: when people received information about child support modifications, how they could submit paperwork while incarcerated, and what other types of decisions they were making at the same time. The focus groups were able to give much needed perspective on this social context, and the team ultimately used these insights to design a more effective intervention. Without taking the time to understand the lived experience of these parents, the intervention that was ultimately designed would have been far less effective.[2]

At this point, research teams should continue considering both individual constraints (cognitive, situational, and process based) *and* broader, structural, and systematic barriers. The practice of overlooking situational constraints may happen during the define stage, as we touched on, but can be most harmful during the traditional discovery stage.

For example, a research team might be brought together to work on decreasing the percentage of mothers in Detroit giving birth early, which increases the health risks faced by mothers and their babies. In a traditional discovery stage, the researchers would not look at racism specifically and instead look at individual mothers' issues. In this traditional version, to understand more about barriers, the researchers might look at administrative data on whether Black mothers are attending prenatal visits. And in fact, the bulk of prior work that has tried unpacking the reasons for increased preterm birth took this traditional approach and was not able to explain the enormous racial disparities.

But in our reimagined stage, researchers would step back and consider broader issues relating to the racism Black mothers in the United States experience. Recent research has taken this approach and unearthed an overlooked factor: the experience of racial discrimination appears to increase negative outcomes for women and their children. Specifically, researchers found that Black women who grew up in the United States are more likely to have negative outcomes during pregnancy compared to African immigrants. However, the daughters of African immigrants experience outcomes that look similar to other Black American women. Income and education don't seem to provide any buffer. It's hypothesized that Black women may be struggling with posttraumatic stress disorder brought on by the chronic stress of facing racial bias in their daily lives.[3] More research will continue to explore the mechanism of this relationship, but in the meantime, mitigating the impacts of everyday racial discrimination may be more important as a public health tool than previously considered. In our context, work begins in this discovery phase by going beyond obvious administrative data, acknowledging that racism may be an underlying factor, and designing formative research to explore the potential connections.

This stage is possibly the most critical (but undervalued) step because it literally defines our understanding of the challenge at hand. In turn, it determines the intervention that is identified, designed, implemented, and evaluated. As we will discuss, many subpar behavioral interventions were the result of a fundamental misunderstanding or oversight during this phase of the process. In other cases, this process was skipped entirely and simply replaced with assumptions.

As in the codefine phase, it's essential that this process be a genuine collaboration so that those who interact most directly with a service, program, or challenge have their perspectives and experiences centered. Here, we describe three strategies that can inform the codefine phase.

ENGAGE IN FORMATIVE RESEARCH

Early in the process, the team should identify the formative research needed to have a nuanced understanding of key decision moments, larger contextual and structural issues, and drop-off points. To gather this information, the team can examine administrative data and conduct literature reviews, focus groups, codesign sessions, and expert interviews. Although qualitative research approaches are often avoided due to time and budget constraints, they're crucial for accurate and inclusive results. Budgets, staff, and timelines should be organized to ensure a healthy formative research phase. This might include earmarking funds for translation services to ensure survey questions are asked in relevant languages, hiring qualitative researchers from the community, and providing financial incentives for survey or focus group participation.

USE PARTICIPATORY RESEARCH METHODS

Participatory action research (PAR)[4] is an effective research approach that involves the direct engagement of impacted communities. PAR provides space for collective inquiry and the evolution of questions of interest by engaging the community as researchers and surveyors.

Mindy learned the value of PAR while doing research in graduate school on ways to help sex workers know their rights. She was working in Kolkata with a grassroots NGO that had very good relationships with the community. Mindy wrote a survey asking sex workers what they knew of local and national legislation that protected them.[5] When Mindy met them and asked the survey questions (through a translator), almost all women reported knowing about their rights.

Looking at the results, the NGO's director laughed and told Mindy that her results were meaningless. The women were not telling Mindy the truth because she was an outsider. This seemed obvious in retrospect. Instead of trying again herself, Mindy recruited and trained three of the teenaged children of the sex workers as codesigners and surveyors. The new surveyors edited the survey, making both the questions and possible responses for multiple choice questions better and more relevant. They also led the survey work themselves. The revised results reflected a more nuanced reality—some women knew some of their rights, and many did not. The experience underlined for Mindy the value of PAR and the enormous risk of launching research without input from the relevant communities: erroneous data and insights.[6]

DON'T BE INTIMIDATED BY THE PAPERWORK REDUCTION ACT

Those who have experience working in the US federal government are likely familiar with the Paperwork Reduction Act (PRA),[7] a critical law that provides some checks and balances on when and how federal agencies collect information and insights from the public. Certain types of information (such as public opinion surveys or large focus groups) require an approval process that can take up to nine months. In our experience, academics and federal partners alike often use PRA as the reason why we *can't* conduct formative research.

Mindy and Crystal remember being in a room with colleagues discussing a project on medication adherence in the United States. They asked if the design team could do some formative interviews with patients. This was a common refrain from us, to the exasperation of many of our colleagues. An academic responded to the question with frustration: "we can't do formative interviews because of PRA, so can we stop talking about it?"

This response was not uncommon, and our colleague was right—PRA is constraining and annoying. But we should stop leaning on it as an excuse to avoid inclusive research. In truth, there are some activities that you can engage in without triggering the cumbersome PRA process. The research team Crystal supported in the BIAS project (mentioned at the start of this chapter) got their insights by designing very small focus groups with parents. The effort was small enough that it didn't require formal review but still yielded incredibly valuable insights.

We don't advocate attempting to circumvent PRA—it serves an incredibly important purpose. Instead, we suggest that the constraints aren't as rigid as often presumed. When working with federal government partners, it's worth learning more about PRA and what you *can* do without engaging in the lengthy review process. And sometimes, the process (and time) may be worth the investment.

A checklist of good antiracist practices at this stage might include the following:

- Valuing mixed methods and investing in experienced qualitative researchers on teams
- Establishing participatory design practices, and allowing the timeline and budget for these practices

- Using formative research tools like surveys and focus groups that intentionally oversample BIPOC populations and are led by and in part designed with BIPOC stakeholders; allocating sufficient budgets to cover staff time from these partner organizations
- Using systems-centered frameworks and language

9 CODESIGN

> If you have come here to help me, you are wasting your time. But if you have come because your liberation is bound up with mine, then let us work together.
> —LILLA WATSON AND ABORIGINAL RIGHTS GROUP OF AUSTRALIA[1]

For many behavioral scientists, the intervention design process is the most exciting stage. So exciting, in fact, that we often jump to this phase without engaging thoughtfully in any of the previous steps. In other contexts, it would be easy to imagine why this is a problem. If a contractor showed up at your door planning to fix your house with only a hammer and a saw, without examining the problem first, you would be concerned. We can use this analogy to understand why a behavioral scientist showing up with a couple of exciting tools without first thoroughly exploring the problem is also problematic.

The goal is to design an intervention that's feasible to implement and test, and that directly addresses the barriers identified during the codiscover phase. An antiracist approach includes defining upstream structural barriers in addition to downstream situational and individual barriers. For example, an intervention with the intermediate goal of increasing the take-up of job training services and the final goal of increasing subsequent employment might note discriminatory hiring practices as a significant institutional barrier. The intervention itself might not be designed to change those barriers, but the research can be designed to identify, expose, and quantify the impact of those upstream barriers.

Crystal's children attend school in the Seattle Public Schools district. Most elementary schools in the district offer a program called Jumpstart that's intended to give incoming kindergartners and their families a chance to connect with the community before the official start of school. The kids have an opportunity to meet their new teacher and classmates, spend time in the building, and start to learn about the school routine. In theory, this is a program with a noble goal: easing the (often difficult) transition for kids and their families.

However, this voluntary program is not equally accessible to all students. Typically, the program runs for several half-days before the start of school. There is no transportation offered, and it's also unclear whether meals or snacks will be offered. A family with a challenging work schedule might not have the ability to drop off and pick up their child—and it's safe to assume that this type of challenge would disproportionately face families of color. At the end of the day, not all families can take advantage of the "jumpstart" offered. A more inclusive approach would be for schools to consult with families (especially those in relatively disadvantaged communities) about what type of program would work best. For example, perhaps a single full-day, instead of several half-days, program that included busing and meals would make it more likely for BIPOC and families experiencing poverty to participate.

DESIGN IN PARTNERSHIP

Traditionally, this phase begins with a small, elite group of folks who work in relative isolation from the targeted population. This may include academic and nonacademic researchers, along with practitioners who may not have frontline experience.

To improve this process, research teams should identify partners who want to engage with key stakeholders. Ideally, these partners were identified early so that in this codesign stage, the team is building on the partnership to consider how to address the issues identified during the discovery phase. Using inclusive design techniques at this stage is important, and there are a few specific methods that can make codesigning successful, described in the following paragraphs.

In-person design workshops can bring together key partners to review formative insights and discuss possible interventions together. This process is often ideal (but not always possible). During our time working with the White House SBST, we remember a large behavioral design workshop we helped to coordinate with partners from three different countries. Each team was made up of a representative from the funding agency (US Agency for International Development), a senior member from the implementing organization (like a health clinic or community organization), and someone from the field, usually a frontline worker. Mindy sat with the group from Nigeria, which included a woman who lived and worked in northern Nigeria where our intervention would take place. She worked in the health clinics, and her perspectives were vital to the design. We would throw out a potential intervention idea, and she would very quickly ground it in the realities of the health clinic. She knew what women in the area would feel comfortable sharing in a survey and what they would not, what modifications clinic staff would accept and what would be too much of a burden, and what data was reliably captured and what data was not. Designing the outlines of a potential intervention in person with someone who had firsthand experience was extremely helpful.

Informational interviews with frontline workers who engage with the population of interest can help researchers receive feedback on the feasibility of potential interventions. Many years ago, as a graduate student, Crystal was designing an intervention to be conducted with soup kitchen patrons. The conversations she had with the staff were essential to her understanding of what would be reasonable and feasible to implement. The staff helped her make decisions about the intervention design (alerting her to potential concerns about privacy but helping her understand that the participants would nonetheless be eager to share their stories) and helping her make decisions about the best way to compensate them for their time (money, gift cards, or other small gifts). Without these insights, the study wouldn't have been successful.[2]

Small-scale pilot testing of interventions with the potential recipients of these interventions with plans to conduct focus groups or interventions to receive feedback is also valuable. Small tests allow for iteration on the intervention before it's launched more widely. And, critically, these small tests can help researchers avoid costly mistakes.

Mindy learned the value of small pilot tests while working on a project in northern Nigeria creating reminders for pregnant women to go to prenatal visits. One hundred percent of women in the study area had never been to school and could not read. The reminder cards needed to be visual, using iconography to get the message across. Mindy designed a card that showed a woman with a growing belly and a fetus inside that grew over time.[3]

The implementing partner had years of experience living and working in northern Nigeria. (Mindy did not.) Although it hadn't occurred to Mindy, local partners insisted that this card be pilot tested with women in the target population. This pilot test turned out to be crucial because women found the image of the fetus creepy and unnerving. Having never been to school, they had never seen an image of a fetus. And, understandably, they were confused by seeing it for the first time. The partners presented a second option, a woman whose belly just grows over time. The women in the focus group enthusiastically preferred that version, and that's the one that was ultimately used. It's possible that if the local partners hadn't piloted the card first, the original reminder card would have been used and could have had the opposite of our desired effect—perhaps women would have simply thrown the cards away because they seemed so strange.

The tactics above cost more, in both time and financial resources, but taking time to fine-tune a potential intervention pays off in the long run.

CONSIDER THE PROPOSED INTERVENTION IN LIGHT OF STRUCTURAL BIASES

At this point, the research team is actively designing an intervention and may be considering a few possible designs. It's essential to consider the role that structural bias might play in each proposed intervention. For example, for decreasing menthol cigarette use in BIPOC communities, it would be important to note that there are intentional forces pushing menthols into BIPOC neighborhoods. The typical behavioral science tactics used to sell cigarettes (use social proof, recruit members of the community as social referents) were compounded by the reality that BIPOC (largely Black) smokers don't see themselves reflected in many public spaces. So glossy images of Black models smoking may have had an especially profound effect.

Therefore, an intervention to decrease use of menthols might leverage insights on corporate tobacco's intentional aim at the Black community by encouraging Black smokers to recognize and fight against predatory marketing by quitting.

We typically engage in the intervention design process by either assuming that no structural bias exists or by acknowledging structural bias but treating it as if it exists outside of the realm of the intervention and study (and is thus ignored). Whether or not it's the intent, the design often assumes that the psychological insights behind the proposed interventions transcend factors like racism.

The psychologists Neil Lewis and Frank Yates describe this effectively and succinctly in their paper describing the success of a University of Michigan program called the Preparation Initiative. They write that "because of this interplay between social structure and psychology, interventions must consider (and potentially simultaneously address) both structural and psychological barriers." The Preparation Initiative is an excellent model of our recommended approach to intervention design. In this program, students from traditionally underrepresented backgrounds are supported in a learning community designed to address a wide range of (individual and systemic) barriers. The blend of components such as individual advising and coaching, structured professional development opportunities, and peer support has been shown to be highly effective and improving both academic success and feelings of belonging.[4]

ANTICIPATE AND DESIGN FOR UNINTENDED CONSEQUENCES

Unintended consequences are often mistakenly labeled as unforeseeable. But they frequently stem from a narrow focus on immediate barriers instead of underlying structural issues. Acknowledging these structural issues early in the design process will help illuminate potential pitfalls and allow researchers to design interventions that address them. In this section, we discuss ways to design an intervention in light of possible unintended consequences, and in chapter 10 we delve into crafting an evaluation plan that can capture downstream effects.

Let's return to our "fan fiction" version of the FAFSA study in chapter 5. When designing interventions to increase applications for financial aid, researchers should have acknowledged some well-documented side effects: that students of color are less likely to *finish* college once they enter and more likely to struggle with loan repayment. An intervention that increases the rate at which they apply for aid (and borrow) risks inadvertently increasing the amount of unmanageable debt BIPOC students of color accrue.

Interventions aimed at increasing FAFSA completion may still be valid and important, but researchers should design the intervention in light of possible downstream consequences. For example (and as laid out in more detail in chapter 5), recognizing that BIPOC borrowers face unique challenges in repaying student loans, researchers could partner with a wider range of organizations—not just tax websites, but also financial empowerment NGOs and relevant universities. The design would aim to help tax filers, especially BIPOC and low-income students, complete not only the FAFSA but also finish postsecondary school with manageable levels of debt. The intervention might still lean into the idea of simplification by using prepopulated tax data to provide potential borrowers with projected debt burdens.

We want to be clear: predicting every potential outcome is impossible. When we drive a car, we don't have perfect visibility—we know there are blind spots. We can't eliminate these entirely, but we can take sensible precautions: checking mirrors and looking over our shoulder before changing lanes. Similarly, some intervention effects are well established and require minimal effort to identify. When we intervene in people's lives, we have a responsibility to do just that—check our mirrors and attempt to identify possible pitfalls and minimize potential harm.

TAKE INSPIRATION FROM OTHER PROGRESSIVE APPROACHES

There are many examples of research that shines light on structural issues, allowing for the consideration of more thorough interventions. For example, in the previous chapter we discussed the emerging evidence connecting the stress of everyday racism to the higher rate of maternal mortality Black mothers experience in the United States. This important work suggests that interventions in this context need to acknowledge structural racism more directly. Attempts to change the practices of health-care providers might be very promising in this regard rather than only focusing on the behavior of the mothers (and implicitly placing the blame squarely on them). For example, as described in the introduction, one recent study showed that access to doula care reduces the rate of cesarean delivery for Medicaid recipients.

A few ambitious interventions have taken a wider lens to incorporate considerations of structural bias. As mentioned earlier, the jigsaw classroom technique successfully uses insights from research on intergroup relations to address and mitigate challenges stemming from racism and discrimination.

A checklist of antiracist practices at this stage might include the following:

- Organizing inclusive codesign sessions
- Creating timelines that allow for iteration after feedback from partners
- Building budgets that allow partners to spend time on design without financial losses
- Being open to a design that likely looks different from the original proposal
- Ensuring evaluation designs have budgets that allow for large and diverse samples and analysis plans that include disaggregation
- Budgeting for intentional time and discussions focused on potential unintended consequences of interventions

10 IMPLEMENT AND INTERPRET

> When we identify where our privilege intersects with somebody else's oppression, we'll find our opportunities to make real change.
>
> —IJEOMA OLUO

Congratulations! With partners, the research team has unpacked underlying barriers to the specific behavioral challenge, conducted a successful design process, and crafted a promising intervention package. The time has come to launch in the field.

The objective of this phase is to implement the intervention as designed and gather and analyze comprehensive insights on how well it's being implemented, outcomes in general and for key populations (e.g., low income, BIPOC), and potential disparities among those populations. As discussed in chapter 4, there are a variety of evaluation methods. RCTs are considered the "gold standard" because they're the best way to know whether it was our intervention (and not something else) that caused the outcome we're interested in. There are times when RCTs are needed, but we must recognize that they can also limit our ability to do good antiracist work.

For example, imagine that the Los Angeles Unified School District (LAUSD) wants to increase reenrollment into the free and reduced-price lunch (FRPL) program. In the codesign and codiscover phase, the district might realize that far more people download the FRPL reenrollment form than complete it. Focus groups tell them that printing and signing a hard copy is a hassle, so they design an intervention making reenrollment possible in a few clicks. They decide on an easy prepost design that compares FRPL reenrollment before and after the intervention. They collect nuanced data, analyze and disaggregate the data, and find that the program increases reenrollment for all students, especially BIPOC. The California Department of Education is impressed with the results of our excellent (imaginary) pilot program and are now contemplating expanding the intervention statewide. To ensure the validity of the results and inform important policy decisions, they want a larger, more robust study on the effects of lunch subsidies on student performance. Fortunately, the intervention is relatively low touch, and the data needed to measure its impact (such as the number of families reenrolling in FRPL) is already reliable and available. So, in this case, conducting an RCT is the right fit.

But randomized experiments are not *always* the right tool. To pursue an antiracist approach to the evaluation of interventions, behavioral scientists should consider how they can supplement experimental methods with other approaches.

RCTs are essential for obtaining robust evidence, but finding adequate sample sizes to complete them can be daunting and sometimes downright infeasible. As a result, when a sizable sample presents itself, behavioral science researchers are quick to seize the opportunity, even if the sample lacks diversity or isn't a precise representation of the community most impacted. This is when we often miss an important opportunity to take an antiracist approach. We assume that our large sample size (which gives us the opportunity to conduct an RCT) will provide insights that we can apply uniformly across diverse and complex populations. We lean on the large sample (and randomization process) to do the work that a more nuanced evaluation approach should do. Behavioral scientists are often reluctant to concede that even with a large sample, important distinctions between (underrepresented) subgroups can be lost.

When designing an RCT, behavioral science researchers tend to prioritize existing, often administrative, data. Consequently, our outcome measures are limited to what is already collected. Remember our efforts to boost bike sharing in big cities across the United States? An intervention that looks at existing riders might skew toward those who are wealthy and white because that's the majority of bike share members. This approach would overlook the experiences of BIPOC individuals who make up a substantial percentage of residents of major cities in the United States but are underrepresented in those cities' bike share programs. An evaluation design that relied on this data might produce a "successful" RCT but also potentially one that fails to capture the diverse experiences of the community.

Imagine that the researchers in the LAUSD study want to see if increased FRPL impacts student success. How would they measure "student success"? The go-to answer is often standardized test scores, but these come with a well-known drawback: standardized tests have been shown to be biased against BIPOC and low-income students.[1] A more comprehensive evaluation might also solicit feedback from teachers, assessing additional factors like student engagement and work quality. This evaluation method might be more expensive, time-consuming, and heavily reliant on strong partnerships with the schools. Importantly, though, it would also offer a more nuanced perspective on the extent to which the intervention was effective for different racial groups.

We aren't advocating that the field move away from RCTs. Instead, we want to acknowledge the limitations of experimental methods (especially those that rely solely on administrative data) and offer strategies that mitigate these limitations. Specifically, more inclusive evaluations will follow two basic principles: (1) intentionally recruit larger and more diverse samples and (2) incorporate qualitative methods to supplement the traditional quantitative approaches used in our work.

Renowned economist John Kenneth Galbraith once said that societies only start solving social problems when they learn how to measure them. So if we want to incite real social change, we must find ways to correctly measure and describe these issues, especially inequality, in all their complexities.

Behavioral scientists can lean on the work of other prominent scholars. In their 2018 book *The Goldilocks Challenge*,[2] Mary Kay Gugerty and Dean Karlan provide a framework that identifies four principles of "right-fit" evaluation approaches for social sector organizations:

- Credible: Data accurately measures what they are supposed to measure, and the analysis produces an accurate result.

- Actionable: Evaluations will generate evidence that can improve the program, and organizations commit to use that evidence regardless of the results.
- Responsible: The benefits of the evaluation outweigh the costs.
- Transportable: Data and insights gleaned from the evaluation can help other programs and decision makers.

Gugerty and Karlan's principles are an excellent start, and behavioral scientists should embrace them. We add the principle of inclusivity to their list:

- Inclusive: The evaluation represents relevant diverse experiences by including large and diverse populations and/or using qualitative methods to shed light on how all communities in the target population are affected.

ENSURE INCLUSIVE EVALUATIONS BY RECRUITING LARGER, MORE DIVERSE SAMPLES

We define race as a social construct, but we also acknowledge, and aim to capture in our research, that racism has devastating impacts on BIPOC lives. As the author and journalist Ta-Nehisi Coates has written, "race is the child of racism, not the father."[3] We want to make sure our studies include diverse populations and that those communities of white, Black, Asian, and Native American individuals are identified and accounted for. This is not because race "explains" behavior, but in recognition that America has manufactured opportunity and deprivation along racial lines. As the Honorable Sonia Sotomayor, US Supreme Court justice, put it, "race matters . . . because of the long history of racial minorities being denied access to the political process . . . [and] persistent racial inequality in society."[4]

We recognize that all evaluations have time, capacity, and budgetary constraints. The inclusivity principle isn't meant to make testing infeasible. Instead, in the design stage, researchers should think about how they'll capture the experiences of key groups within the larger population. They can let the relevant context dictate what groups will be most important to study. This means budgeting the time, money, and staff to recruit a large and diverse sample. Since most behavioral research depends on funding, private and federal funders can play a role in pushing this more nuanced research forward by providing funding with longer time frames and bigger budgets to allow for partnership development and additional formative research. (We offer specific suggestions to funders in chapter 11).

Consider the illustrative FRPL study in LA and assume that to see a difference in FRPL reenrollment, the researchers need a total sample of one thousand students. At this point, the research team should explicitly discuss important populations they'll want to know more about. For example, let's say the FRPL study is being piloted in two schools with large white, Latino, and Black populations and researchers want to be sure they are able to understand how the form change impacted these families specifically. Rather than relying on *post hoc* analyses of differences across these racial groups, minimal detectable difference calculations should be done *before* recruitment for each of these groups. Assuming an appropriate percentage of loss, now how many Black, Latino, and white students need to be recruited? Partnerships will help as organizations close to the community can assist with recruitment and retention to ensure that studies successfully recruit adequate numbers of study participants from key communities.

CONDUCT NUANCED DISAGGREGATION

As research teams plan to capture an intervention's impact on key communities, they should also design the evaluation to capture relevant variance *within* those communities. For example, thinking about richly varied BIPOC populations as one broad demographic group like Black or Latino will provide some insights on how an intervention affected different groups (and collecting that data is usually straightforward and easy to code). But these blanket categories can obscure shades of differences in skin tone and treatment *within* those groups. A white Latina will have different—and research tells us, more positive—interactions in school, with the police, and in seeking employment than her dark-skinned cousin. And yet, almost all behavioral interventions would group these two individuals, and analyze their behavior, under one "Latino" (or even "non-white") umbrella.

As social scientists, we should know that there is a deep bench of research demonstrating the impact of colorism, or discrimination based on skin tone: darker-skinned individuals (whether African American, Latino, or mixed), on average, make less money, live in more segregated areas, and are more likely to be arrested than those with similar backgrounds but with lighter skin. The color of their skin can influence people's lives on almost any social outcome we track, yet the field consistently fails to consider colorism or collect relevant data to better understand its impact. This oversight means that our designs consistently neglect a major structural barrier, and our results fail to account for skin tone stratification.

Why is this critical? Imagine an intervention aimed at decreasing disruptive behavior in schools. A reasonable study design might examine suspension rates before and after the intervention, with researchers collecting data across racial and ethnic categories. However, also collecting self-reported skin color would make the results more useful. Multiple studies have found that even when controlling for parental income, delinquent behavior, academic performance, and several other variables, darker-skinned Black students are far more likely to be suspended.[5] Failure to consider this nuance could confuse and misrepresent the study's findings and implications. In this hypothetical example, the research team would want to design around the insight that the unconscious bias of teachers and administrators might impact suspensions. If the intervention can't be designed to address this bias, it should at least be designed to capture, quantify, and expose this bias.

To do this, researchers should plan to gather nuanced data, including relevant variables like skin tone. Skin color is now collected in several large-scale surveys, including the General Social Survey, the National Longitudinal Survey of Youth, the American National Election Studies, and the Latin American Public Opinion Project's AmericasBarometer study. The instruments used in these surveys should be considered by others looking to include skin color in their analyses.[6] (A link to the instrument used by the National Longitudinal Survey of Youth is included in the resources section.)

Gathering this type of nuanced data is incredibly valuable, but it's also time-consuming and not always relevant to the research question at hand. We don't want to imply that researchers must collect data on every demographic variable possible. Instead, it's important to let the practical or policy context dictate what matters most. Defining the possible racialized factors impacting behavior change and engaging partners with lived experience in the behavioral challenge will help determine which demographic variables are most relevant.

USE AN INTERSECTIONAL APPROACH

The civil rights leader and scholar Kimberlé Crenshaw coined the term intersectionality, which she describes as "a metaphor for understanding the ways that multiple forms of inequality or disadvantage sometimes compound themselves and create obstacles that often are not understood among conventional ways of thinking."[7]

Exploring overlapping identities can reveal deeper relationships that cannot be adequately understood by considering demographic groupings independently. Scholars who work on intersectionality point to two main goals of the intersectionality framework: (1) it seeks to understand the unique experiences at the nexus of multiple social positions of power, and (2) its application to research should be done to advance social justice. As Crenshaw explained, "the better we understand how identities and power work together from one context to another, the less likely our movements for change are to fracture.[8]"

Let's see how this looks in practice. Researchers decided to dive deeper into suspension data for Black students by looking at both gender and skin color. This deeper inspection revealed that the overall finding regarding the higher rates of suspension for darker-skinned Black students was actually driven by the experiences of female students. The odds of suspension were about three times greater for young Black women with the darkest skin tone compared to those with the lightest. These insights bring up important questions for a research team: what barriers are dark-skinned young women in schools facing? What preconceived notions do teachers and school administrators hold about these young women? And most importantly, how can an intervention help?

An intervention designed to name and respond to these questions will be more impactful and more accurate. But first, nuanced demographic data must be collected and merged to explore important intersecting identities. For example, regression models can use interaction terms to explore how an intervention impacted light and dark skinned Black male students, light and dark skinned Black female students, and white students. Multivariable regression techniques for intersectional analysis can help research teams identify the combined effect of multiple intersecting identities on outcomes while also accounting for other factors.

In the resources section, we provide useful guides from the US government and public health scholars detailing useful methods for analyzing intersectionality in quantitative research.

LEVERAGE QUALITATIVE METHODS

In many cases, it simply may not be possible to recruit a large BIPOC sample. Other times, recruitment efforts simply fail to secure a diverse sample. For an intervention that impacts BIPOC communities, it's not enough to forge ahead, ignoring entire communities, and then write up results and say "not enough is known about the impact of subpopulations. More research is needed."

Frankly, almost every researcher has been guilty of writing a version of the sentence above—us included. But we need to do better. Let's say finding a sample of BIPOC participants large enough to be statistically significant isn't possible. Researchers could hold a focus group with BIPOC participants to gather insights on their experiences. The results of the focus group should also be presented alongside the experiment's results (and not shunted off to the appendix).

Recall the doll study from chapter 1. The Clarks's work had a small sample size (only three hundred children), but it helped lead to the *Brown v. Board of Education* Supreme Court ruling that racial segregation in public education was unconstitutional. Despite its small sample size, the study's findings were too consequential to be brushed aside.

Their work has since been replicated. While the sample sizes are still very modest, watching the original and updated videos of young Black children repeatedly pointing to the Black doll as the one that is bad, not pretty and not nice, leaves the viewer with a visceral (and heartbreaking) appreciation of the destructive impact of discrimination.

USE ADMINISTRATIVE DATA CREATIVELY

Behavioral scientists value administrative data like test scores or attendance records, but these traditional metrics of intervention "success" may not provide crucial nuance into how to interpret the impacts of an intervention. Consider again the hypothetical LAUSD study. Less hunger and more food due to reenrollment in the FRPL program might indeed help BIPOC students focus in class. But standardized tests are a lagging indicator that is unlikely to pick up this impact. Could student engagement be a better outcome to track? If so, researchers need to consider ways to collect the right data to capture engagement over time. Do teachers complete routine student evaluations that could be analyzed? A process like this would certainly require more effort than downloading test scores, but it might be a feasible metric to collect and provide more valuable insight into the intervention's effect.

A study by the applied economist Lisa Gennetian and colleagues provides an instructive illustration of how collecting nontraditional metrics of school success can reveal new insights.[9] Her research team studied students from families receiving Supplemental Nutrition Assistance Program (SNAP) and found that disciplinary incidents at school spiked at the end of the benefit cycle. Families are likely to be stretched thin by the end of month, leading to hunger and stress and potentially affecting students' overall mood and behavior. The connection between hunger and student behavior raises important questions about the role of nutrition and access to food on students' well-being, extending beyond their academic performance. Leveraging nontraditional metrics helped uncover a deeper story.

WHEN POSSIBLE, PLAN TO IDENTIFY POTENTIAL UNINTENDED AND DOWNSTREAM CONSEQUENCES

Cocreating an evaluation design to identify an intervention's impact can also help identify any unintended consequences. For example, in our hypothetical intervention to increase biking in DC, working with a local NGO in the design stage might unearth Black men's concern of increased police profiling and violence. As a result, the study design would include focus groups or surveys with Black men in the study, specifically asking whether increased use of bike share increased police interactions.

Research teams should actively consider how structural factors (e.g., bias in lending, stigma, or stereotypes) might dictate additional outcome measures to be collected. In a recent piece discussing the need for a more thorough integration of social psychology into the use of behavioral insights for public policy, Crystal and her colleague Ines Jurcevic explore the idea of "psychological taxes."[10] Far too often, behavioral scientists ignore the fact that our interventions may have psychological impacts that we fail to acknowledge or measure. Leveraging insights from social psychology will help research teams explore possible psychological taxes.

For example, in the FAFSA study mentioned earlier, we discuss the unintended consequence of BIPOC study participants taking on unmanageable debt. Burdensome debt is one obvious unintended consequence. But the evaluation could be designed to address more subtle consequences of taking out a college loan, such as stress and regret. Scholars Jalil B. Mustaffa and Jonathan Davis surveyed Black borrowers about their experiences taking out college loans. Considering unintended consequences, they asked borrowers, "In retrospect, do you regret having taken out student loans to fund your education?" Almost 70 percent reported that yes, they did regret taking out their loans.[11]

It's also important to consider that interventions that emphasize a particular stigma (perhaps one's own immigration status) may trigger negative emotions, which in turn may deplete cognitive resources. Imagine a researcher is designing a communication intervention with parents who are undocumented to encourage take-up of a free vaccination program for their children. The communication campaign might underline that people who are undocumented are invited to the clinic and that immigration status should not stop anyone from getting vaccinated. These parents might be compelled to participate in the clinic (assuming it's an effective intervention), but they also might experience some negative mental health impacts because the communication campaign acknowledged their immigration status. The researchers might note that their intervention "worked," and vaccinations increased, but they would fail to note other potential consequences. Perhaps these parents might now be *less* likely to take other actions that continue to emphasize their stigmatized identity, or experience additional stress or anxiety after engaging in the program. At this stage, researchers could consider both the behavioral *and* the psychological impacts of the intervention by intentionally gathering data on post-intervention vaccination behavior and self-reported anxiety resulting from the letter campaign.

BUDGET ADEQUATE RESOURCES TO EXECUTE THE EVALUATION

Organizations reveal their values by their budgets. The same is true for examining whether an applied behavioral science endeavor aims to be antiracist. Executing antiracist evaluations will require more time and resources than traditional evaluations.

If the team decides qualitative data collection is essential, resources to support it should be intentionally written into the intervention design. This means allocating the time and budget for focus groups, interviews, or surveys and recruiting research staff with experience in these methods.

At a broader level, Institutional Review Board processes and requests for proposals from funders could build inclusivity into their templates by considering how the research will capture the experiences of relevant marginalized communities. For example, in 2021 the NIH Brain Research through Advancing Innovative Neurotechnologies (BRAIN) initiative created a funding opportunity that requires research proposals to include a "Plan for Enhancing Diverse Perspectives (PEDP)."[12] That plan is scored and reviewed as part of the award process. Requiring projects that impact BIPOC populations to detail their plan to include BIPOC perspectives specifically would take this effort one step further.

A checklist of good antiracist practices at this stage might include the following:

- Collecting larger samples with significant BIPOC representation
- Collecting and analyzing diverse demographic data, including nuanced variables like skin tone
- Taking an intersectional approach by analyzing how disempowered identities (female, Latino, dark skinned) might interact and influence an intervention
- Hiring and budgeting for qualitative research
- Extending project time horizons to allow for identifying and collecting data on unintended consequences

11 SHARE, ADAPT, AND SCALE

I would give
to the human race
only hope.

I am the woman
offering two flowers
whose roots
are twin

Justice and Hope
Hope and Justice

Let us begin.

—ALICE WALKER

The intervention has been successfully launched, and the researchers have been dutifully collecting and analyzing the resulting qualitative and quantitative data. Now the goal is to document the success (or not!) of the intervention. Did the intervention work, for whom, and what should people learn from it? During this step, there are a few important ways we currently fall short.

Traditionally, results are written up and shared internally with an organization and externally in a trade or academic publication. Usually only the researchers have a role in the analysis and final presentation, and we typically focus on publishing findings in academic journals or policy reports and sharing them at professional meetings or conferences. It's uncommon for researchers to share even applied research findings with the communities who are intended to benefit from them. This oversight means we miss insights on the results, ideas for application, and ways to improve our interventions in the future.

When our positive results are presented, the intervention's impacts are typically presented as *general* impacts on the full sample and then, only sometimes, by subgroups. Because BIPOC samples are often small and lack statistical power (due to oversight at the evaluation design stage), many studies will report general results without ever discussing differential impacts. In other words, because the field usually fails to plan for and collect sufficient samples of BIPOC participants, we often don't know if these communities experienced the intervention in a different way than the population as a whole.

One (admittedly small) adjustment to small BIPOC samples is to add statistical power by merging BIPOC groups together into one and presenting results of "non-white" populations in the main report and then presenting results by each demographic group in the appendix (where authors may note that because groups are small, these results do not meet statistical significance). We have both presented data this way many times. It is an understandable workaround when the sample of BIPOC is not large enough to consider ethnic groups in a more nuanced way. But it's also problematic because ethnic groups are internally and externally diverse.

Crystal regularly teaches an introductory statistics course to students of public policy, and she finds it telling that these students are quite adept at quickly identifying the problems with this approach from a policy perspective. They formulate policy-driven research questions and attempt analytic approaches with the intent of understanding the nuance among communities of color—rather than simply comparing them, in one large group, to white folks. In contrast, seasoned behavioral scientists tend to accept the limitations of small sample sizes of BIPOC groups rather than fundamentally challenging why these small sample sizes exist in the first place.

Once results are collected, analyzed, and shared, the hope is that successful interventions will be scaled. In fact, one of the most exciting underlying promises of applied behavioral science is the potential for low-cost, high-impact interventions to be scaled to thousands or even millions. And a few well-known interventions have indeed taken off at scale.

The FAFSA study discussed earlier that prepopulated as much information as possible from preexisting tax information increased financial aid applications and college-going among low-income students. A simplification approach was later folded into the 2020 US FAFSA Simplification Act, and as a result, this intervention has reached millions.[1] Similarly, studies around making a plan to vote have taken off and are now used as standard get-out-the-vote techniques by both political parties. These are two success stories that provide a narrative that most applied behavioral scientists strive for: rigorous experimental research being used for larger-scale change in large, consequential contexts.

While rolling out a behavioral intervention on a massive scale is an exciting opportunity to expand the reach of an effective insight, it also has the potential to be high consequence for communities that might have been overlooked in the original research. As we have mentioned already, unintentional, negative outcomes in a small study snowball on a national scale. Happily, the opposite is also true. If a racist practice has been exposed in the research, when the study is scaled and publicized, that issue can also be brought to light, with the potential for reform and advocacy. We present some approaches to disseminating results that center inclusive methods.

USE A PARTICIPATORY PROCESS TO ANALYZE RESULTS AND PRESENT RECOMMENDATIONS

Sometimes, researchers will share the results of a study with the community for informational purposes, essentially to "update" the community. Going further, results can be shared to both inform and improve the research itself. For example, a Data Walk is a tool from the Urban Institute that shares data and research findings with stakeholders.[2] During a Data Walk, stakeholders divide into small groups and visit "stations" that tell a story about the research in accessible ways, allowing community participants to review, analyze, and suggest improvements. On a technical level, this approach can ensure a more robust analysis and understanding of the data. In terms of power dynamics and respect, this type of engagement allows researchers and community members to create meaning and solutions together, moving our field toward respectful partnership and away from the traditional paradigm in which communities are subjects who are "studied." Whatever the method, the goal should be to share and analyze results with relevant stakeholders before publication.

DISCUSS RESULTS WITH AS MUCH NUANCE AS POSSIBLE

Prior to this step, research teams have ideally collected large and diverse samples and used qualitative methods to capture additional nuance. At this stage, researchers can dip into their rich data to tease out diverse impacts and share those perspectives in the final write-up.

When relevant, results should be presented by racial subgroups (e.g., Latino, Black, Asian, white, multiracial) by ethnicity (e.g., Puerto Rican, Cuban, Chinese, Thai), and, when relevant, by skin tone. Researchers should also consider using intersectional analyses (as discussed in chapter 9). Because it's almost never feasible to present every possible sociodemographic variable, we urge research teams to carefully examine the policy context and make reasonable decisions about what variables should be reported.

If the sample size is too small to reach statistical significance, race and ethnicity data can be presented descriptively, and qualitative methods like case studies can be used to detail different experiences and potential impacts, even if the statistical argument is weak. As a field, this would be the norm if we valued understanding marginalized experiences as much as we value statistical significance. Reporting the results by demographic groups might also help motivate future research to take a more deliberate look at findings across racially and ethnically diverse populations.

Researchers should note that it can be challenging to know the most appropriate way to create subgroups. The breakdown of people of color in the United States, for example, should likely be different than in the United Kingdom or Canada. The definition of these racial and ethnic groups will constitute significant work, and this process should be given appropriate time and resources to be done well.

IDENTIFY AND DISCUSS RELEVANT STRUCTURAL BIASES

When we sidestep systemic issues in our publications, we conceal deeper injustices and feed the story that BIPOC struggles are self-inflicted. It's like pointing to faulty branches while ignoring the rotted roots below. After George Floyd's murder, the economist William Spriggs articulated this frustration in the field of economics: "The fact that far too many economists blindly agree that negative attributes correlate to being African American and cannot see that relationship to police officers assuming all Black men are criminals is stupefying. The fact that a discipline that prides itself on being objective and looking for data to test hypotheses fails to see how negative attributes do not correlate with being African American is a constant irritant for Black economists."

The economist Andre Perry makes a related observation in his 2020 book exploring the extensive negative impacts of the systematic and deliberate devaluation of Black communities.[3] In his introduction, he provides a critique of how traditional methods in the field of economics are inadequate for studying the impacts of racism. He writes that "historical discrimination categorically leveled against Black people makes it difficult for many research projects to make a true apples-to-apples comparison with White people. For instance, to compare a Black person's income to that of a White person without accounting for the wealth that was systematically denied to Black people by federal policy is to bury one's head in the sand and ignore the roles of racism and White Privilege. Racism is a common denominator for Black people; it's a given." He goes on to describe how an examination of differences within Black communities is better at helping to understand the mechanisms of wealth differences.

At the moment, researchers, and the journal editors and reviewers who control research publications, aren't accustomed to framing results in structural terms. But we can change this.

Though the intervention may not have targeted racial structures directly, naming them in the final publication raises awareness and informs future research. By acknowledging structural racism in our findings and their implications, we contribute to ongoing efforts to address systemic racism.

An excellent recent publication (mentioned earlier in this book) led by the scholar NiCole T. Buchanan provides an actionable set of strategies to address and combat systemic racism in the research practices of psychological science.[4] The authors provide clear suggestions on how to report psychological findings more effectively, with a focus on antiracism. For example, just as we propose using systems-centered frameworks to define the behavioral challenge (in chapter 6), writers ought to use systems-centered language when drafting results to clearly identify relevant institutions and systems that act as barriers.

To see what this looks like in practice, there are several articles and papers about child and maternal mortality rates that frame the issue as some version of "Black mothers and children at risk of death during childbirth." In contrast, a recent *New York Times* article on a similar topic used systems-centered language to place the issue in a broader context.[5] The headline was "Racism and Sexism Underlie Higher Maternal Death Rates for Black Women, UN Says." The systems language puts the findings squarely in the context of disempowerment.

WITH PARTNERS, DECIDE HOW TO SHARE RESULTS IN DIVERSE, ACCESSIBLE OUTLETS AND FORMATS

All partners in a research project should collaborate on decisions regarding where, how, and when to present and share results. While all stakeholders may not (and should not) be formal researchers, they can play a role in deciding how best to share results with different audiences. Instead of a sole focus on academic publications and technical reports, findings can be shared in blog posts, podcasts, videos, and infographics that are designed to speak to different audiences. When sharing results with news outlets, we should look beyond the usual elite newspapers and magazines and share our work with smaller outlets that reach local communities.

Crystal had the privilege of working on a University of Washington project examining mobility challenges faced by youth living in a majority BIPOC neighborhood in South Seattle. The team was interdisciplinary and diverse. It included scholars from departments across the university, along with community leaders and activists, and prioritized participatory methods and a focus on mobility justice. Researchers and community leaders worked together to decide where and how to share the results. Not surprisingly, they were shared using atypical methods for academic studies. An accessible website was created to share information about the research, including photos, videos, and a creative infographic. And the team conducted a community forum to share and discuss the findings. Some members of the team also published op-eds in a range of local news outlets.[6]

Engaging in research in this way was an exciting new experience. Crystal loved that the community was involved at every stage of the research—the team's principal investigators were models of active listening and centering the lived experience of the population of interest. Even as the project's implementation got stalled by the COVID-19 pandemic, the team prioritized learning how to make the research questions, methodology, and dissemination engaging and relevant to the South Seattle community. This was most evident in the participation of community members in the forum to discuss the findings.

Moving further from research to advocacy, researchers can intentionally partner with advocacy organizations to share findings that can arm activists with data and insights to help in their work pushing for more equitable policy and programming.[7]

In addition, journal submission portals can provide more inclusive journal keywords to indicate that research on diversity, equity, and inclusion is valued. As researchers, it's important that we don't assume research results speak on their own. By making our results more accessible to a general audience, our findings can reach more people, increasing the potential for impact on real-world problems and informing the next wave of research questions.

ENSURE DISSEMINATION EVENTS INCLUDE BIPOC SPEAKERS AND REACH BIPOC AUDIENCES

When researchers touch on subjects that impact BIPOC populations, researchers should ensure that dissemination events include diverse speakers and reach diverse audiences. This may require time to develop partnerships and relationships with relevant organizations. In addition, hosting more inclusive events may likely incur new costs, like honorariums for guest speakers or grants to BIPOC organizations that may cohost and codesign the dissemination event. Institutions like the Urban Institute and the London School of Economics have created event guidelines to help researchers plan and execute inclusive dissemination events.[8] Guidance includes tips like ensuring diversity not just of speakers but also of event organizers, thinking beyond classic large informal presentations to smaller, more local events, and providing childcare for parents, especially mothers, whose attendance is often limited due to care responsibilities.

A checklist of good antiracist practices at this stage might include the following:

- Adjusting timelines and budgets to ensure that results can be shared, analyzed, and adjusted when needed with relevant stakeholders before publication.
- Exploring differential impacts with nuance. This might include presenting qualitative findings and analyzing impacts by ethnicity, skin color, or an intersectional approach that looks at the interaction of multiple identities.
- Training staff in systems-centered language and frameworks so that results can be discussed considering systemic issues rather than individual weaknesses.
- Recognizing all partners who made significant contributions as coauthors (not only prioritizing academic authors).
- Working with partners to find diverse and inclusive venues for sharing research results and receiving feedback on findings.

12 ACTION AGENDA

> Power concedes nothing without a demand. It never did and it never will.
> —FREDERICK DOUGLASS

Updating our current practices to ones that actively confront racism will involve more than a few tweaks and nudges. The good news is that plenty can be done *right now*. In this final section, we detail specific and actionable recommendations for five key groups: academic gatekeepers (academics and their institutions, journal reviewers and editors, etc.), students, funders, practitioners and policymakers, and behavioral science consumers.

Whereas the other chapters talk about what can be done before and during a specific project, these recommendations are aimed at shaping an enabling environment that can support antiracist behavioral science.

FOR ACADEMICS

Much effort lies ahead for those who engage in this work in the halls of academia, but senior scholars and journal editors have the most crucial role. As a first step, senior academics must update hiring, promotion, and tenure processes; the way young scholars are trained; and the makeup of editorial boards.

In the United States, 6 percent of university faculty members are Latino and 5 percent are Black, although Latinos make up almost 19 percent of the population, and 13 percent of the population identifies as Black.[1] We need to do better, and we can start by recruiting BIPOC talent early. Universities can reach out to HBCUs, TCUs, and students of color organizations at traditional colleges to recruit students and staff as well as offer internships. Universities can ensure there are recruitment and admissions staff who are BIPOC and provide financial aid for BIPOC populations.

The American Psychological Foundation's Minority Fellowship Program (MFP) Fund for Racial and Ethnic Diversity is an instructive example of concrete steps universities can take to hire and support BIPOC scholars.[2] The MFP funds fellowships, research, training, and mentorship, and it helps to address the lack of diversity in the mental health and allied fields. Hosting events for prospective BIPOC students can be especially impactful. When visiting prospective graduate programs, Crystal was highly influenced by the students of color events at Princeton University. It was there that she connected with other Black prospective psychology doctoral students—all of whom accepted their offers of admission, and as a result formed an entering cohort with four (out of only nine total!) Black students in the department.

Once they're hired, promotion systems should support scholars aiming to address racism in their work. Currently, promotions are closely tied to publishing. That process, and the rough road to publication, means that a scholar taking an antiracist approach to their work will have more to do (recruiting more diverse samples, spending time cultivating diverse partnerships, leading rich qualitative research, sharing results in wider, untraditional ways) and therefore may struggle to meet publishing demands.

In recognition of this, hiring and promotion processes should consider the extent to which scholars' work acknowledges, challenges, and addresses racism (along with other equity issues). Engaging in deep and meaningful partnerships with a wide range of partners (especially those *outside* of academia) is challenging. The act of doing so—and being able to communicate this scholarship effectively to both academics and nonacademics—must be given higher value. Unfortunately, as it stands, the perceived lack of "credit" for this type of work far too often results in young scholars believing they must leave academia altogether. Crystal has had several dear friends and colleagues (scholars of color) leave tenure-track positions because they felt they couldn't engage in the work they were most passionate about in the confines of those positions. Many institutions are attempting to codify language and policies on how contributions to equity and inclusion should be considered in hiring and promotion, but much work remains.

Academics must also reimagine the way that young scholars are trained. For example, behavioral scientists should have more exposure to qualitative methods. Even if they don't reach expert status, they should be able to recognize the value of qualitative research to complement experimental approaches. Many of the most impactful work in the field takes a mixed methods approach. Unfortunately, qualitative methods are almost never required for students learning behavioral science (at both the master's and doctoral level)—and often are not even offered as an option.

Behavioral science students who want to focus on issues in the United States could also be introduced to courses that provide a strong theoretical and practical foundation in why and how race influences almost all the behaviors they, as applied behavioral scientists, will try to influence. Race-conscious frameworks like critical race theory[3] and targeted universalism[4] can provide critical perspectives that challenge the status quo, giving young scholars a much-needed race-aware perspective to use in their research questions and study designs. Additionally, endorsing and training students in other strategies such as citation audits[5] ensures that authors actively diversify the race and ethnicity of scholars cited within their research groups and individual papers. Engaging in more general discussions of how to disrupt white-centered[6] research practices will also be essential. The Society for Personality and Social Psychology has offered workshops in both practices, and it's time for the broader behavioral science community to follow suit.

The recent open science movement will also act in the service of antiracism by making methods, materials, and unpublished reports more readily available to nonacademic partners and communities, along with encouraging thoughtful study replication. This is important because these practices will make it easier to identify precisely *when* our interventions work and *for whom*. Gatekeepers in the field have the opportunity and responsibility to keep up a steady drumbeat in its favor, including training young scholars in open science practices.

As discussed in chapter 2, we also need more journals and conferences that provide platforms for researchers to present new research on the intersection of racism and behavioral science. In our search of both general and field-specific academic databases, journals that looked at race and behavioral science made up only about 0.4 percent of the total. And while sister fields like sociology and economics have established conferences and platforms dedicated to exploring racism and inequality, we could find only one similar conference in the applied behavioral sciences.

Finally, we need to work toward diverse editorial boards. In a recent study, researchers Sakaria L. Auelua-Toomey and Steven O. Roberts provided experimental evidence suggesting that the racial makeup of an editorial board impacts whether scholars who study race believe the journal values and would publish their work and whether or not they would submit work to that journal. Further, they found that all scholars (those who do and do not study race) had more positive perceptions of journals with more diverse editorial boards.[7]

Intentionally recruiting BIPOC scholars to sit on editorial boards will meet resistance. Crystal recently spent several years as the chair of the first-ever Diversity and Inclusion Committee for the Society of Judgment and Decision Making (one of her primary academic professional affiliations). Despite the commitments leaders in the field have made, there is still significant friction around engaging in efforts to actively recruit more underrepresented students of color and to create spaces only for scholars of color. There's a tendency to approach these discussions as zero-sum—that some will be "left out" when we intentionally reach out to scholars of color. This must evolve. These positions (of, ironically, wanting to create space for "everyone") are often put forth as principled, but they create deep harm by alienating scholars of color, making their recruitment and retention in academia even more difficult.

FOR STUDENTS

Students at undergraduate and graduate levels can help build demand for antiracist behavioral research by advocating for the recommendations above.

For example, students can ask professors to explore systemic barriers to the behavioral challenges being discussed and challenge the dominant focus on individual-level behavior change. They can organize and call on administrations to offer courses in race-conscious frameworks like critical race theory and targeted universalism. And they should urge their professors and administrators to discuss qualitative and participatory research methods and organize to ensure that courses on these methods are offered.

Finally, students can help petition universities to ensure there are BIPOC perspectives on faculty. Numerous student-led efforts can act as guides. For example, in 2016 the University of California Los Angeles (UCLA) Black Graduate Student Association launched an initiative aimed to increase the number of Black faculty members and included a petition, rallies, and meetings with university administrators. The university pledged to do better, and it did: in 2016, the university had forty-eight tenured or tenure-track Black faculty members, a number that had remained largely stagnant for several years. By 2020, that number had increased to seventy-one, representing a 48 percent increase over four years.[8]

FOR FUNDERS

Private and government funding often functions like an urban planner in the research landscape, shaping the rules and structures that influence the way science is practiced. By providing researchers with significant funding and proactive support, funders can build a sturdy foundation for antiracist initiatives and research practices.

Funders have come a long way since the early 2000s, when the vice president of a large foundation told Mindy that "we don't say 'race and class' at this foundation."[9] The events of 2020 pushed funders to recognize the role of race and racism in American life. Now, the funding community (both government funders and private philanthropy) needs to match their public commitments to racial justice with concrete investments. As mentioned in chapter 2, our research reveals a scarcity of funding opportunities focused on racial equity and systemic racism. Only 1 percent of NSF and 2 percent of APA funding opportunities address these issues. Within NSF divisions, we found only one grant in behavioral and cognitive sciences and exactly zero grant opportunities focused on racial equity in the social and economic sciences.

In addition to providing financial resources, funders should name that the broad goal of equity will require specifically focusing on racial justice, significantly investing in antiracist work, rethinking traditional timelines, designing grant opportunities that ensure collaboration with BIPOC communities, and recruiting staff with racial and ethnic backgrounds that reflect the communities impacted by their funding.

There is an opportunity for funders to be thought leaders in this space. Darren Walker, one of the few Black foundation heads and president of the Ford Foundation, has been an instructive guide. The foundation makes their commitment to fighting structural racism clear. For example, they not only funded research on the racial wealth gap but also described it by saying "the racial wealth gap is a structural and historical problem, not primarily an individual one. So, our boldest solutions need to be structural too."[10] This is clear, systems-centered language that all applied behavioral scientists should practice.

As they work to live out their own commitments to antiracism, funders should be led by the insight that *budgets reveal values of organizations*. Again, Ford provides a strong model. The foundation backed up their commitment to the fight for racial justice with significant investments. In 2020, when most foundations were worried about their endowments, the Ford Foundation sold $1 billion in social bonds to have more liquid for grantmaking. With the resulting income, Ford doubled their funding for US-based racial justice and civil rights groups. They've also extended their impact by asking other foundations and philanthropists to join them. As Darren Walker said in 2021 when asked about Ford's increased investment in racial justice, "my challenge to philanthropy is that we have to do more . . . this post-COVID world requires us to go beyond our usual practices."

An aspect of the usual practice is rushed research due to deadlines and demands associated with small budgets and unrealistic time frames, which makes every part of an antiracist behavioral design process difficult. It's hard to partner with and recruit diverse researchers, conduct good formative research, and recruit large and diverse samples on a too-tight time frame.

Funders can support more inclusive design processes by covering the costs of longer timelines, hiring qualitative researchers, and supporting staff at BIPOC NGOs who can be implementation and thought partners. To do even more, funders can design grant opportunities that specifically solicit behavior change research with antiracist methods and goals. As previously mentioned, in 2021 the NIH BRAIN initiative published "RFA-MH-21–180," a bureaucratic-sounding title for an inclusive funding innovation. The funding opportunity requires research proposals to include a "Plan for Enhancing Diverse Perspectives (PEDP)," which are scored and reviewed as part of the award process.[11]

FOR PRACTITIONERS AND POLICYMAKERS

Practitioners and policymakers in governments and nonprofits have been essential to the widespread use of behavioral science for the public good; these partnerships make the implementation of behavioral interventions possible. As the field continues to evolve, their role will need to adapt as well—indeed, their evolution will push us forward.

Government partners can help researchers access both the quantitative and qualitative data they need to create an inclusive evaluation. This might mean helping researchers collect better demographic data by adding a "race/ethnicity" question on a current form or supporting qualitative evaluation even when it may trigger the PRA. These relatively small efforts can have outsized impacts. For example, many of the invaluable insights on the impacts of colorism in America are the direct result of government agencies like the Bureau of Labor Statistics adding a question about skin color to one of their surveys. And because a few of the government surveys that added skin tone color questions were longitudinal, researchers have been able to study how the impacts of colorism have evolved over time.

Government collaborators can also help bring the right people to the table by coordinating meetings, interviews, and focus groups with frontline workers and the people they serve. When we worked with the former White House SBST, one refrain was that when planning a project, there were two crucial people to have in the room: the person with the power to approve the study or intervention and the person who would ultimately be responsible for implementation. While this makes sense in terms of immediate efficiency, it's ultimately shortsighted since it leaves out representatives from the community. Because our government partners are often white and the communities we're working with are so often BIPOC, it creates an unchallenged, white-centered dynamic. Practitioners and government partners have the power to actively and thoughtfully address this shortcoming.

Finally, government partners can set the policy priorities that shape the way resources are deployed to gather and use scientific evidence in pursuit of social justice. And with the 2021 and 2023 executive orders on advancing racial equity, government partners now also have the duty to do so. For example, to make sharing data between government agencies easier, the Office of Management and Budget could create guidelines that facilitate data sharing between agencies. Making data sharing easier allows agencies that don't usually collect data about race or ethnicity to work with those that do. In a recent report, the Urban Institute detailed specific ways the federal government can invest in data accessibility in order to realize the goals of 2021 and 2023 executive orders, including establishing an Office of Data Equity to support the Census Bureau, providing more funding to embed statisticians in US agencies to facilitate nuanced equity analyses, and exploring new data sources and methods, including private-sector data and imputation, to enhance data disaggregation by race and ethnicity.[12]

Research and policy organizations can invest in initiatives that focus specifically on structural racism or create cross-cutting initiatives that integrate an antiracist perspective into each key research area. To do this well, organizations should prioritize hiring staff with relevant lived experience and provide training, tools, and incentives for staff to learn more about antiracism and engage in advancing racial justice in their work.

FOR BEHAVIORAL SCIENCE FANS AND HOBBYISTS

Finally, we encourage the growing number of people around the world who could be described as "behavioral science curious" to view themselves less as consumers of behavioral science and more as agents of change. We need this influential community to approach new insights with healthy skepticism and an eye toward the principles of antiracism. Crystal has been struck that her master's students often provide the most significant opportunities for her to explore her own doubts. Instead of taking the lessons from the field as gospel, they ask hard questions and challenge the assumptions that many behavioral scientists take for granted.

Fans of behavioral science can do the same. For example, when learning about a particular intervention or experiment, outsiders can challenge the extent to which a research team engaged in good antiracist practices and ask if communities with lived experience were consulted. Call researchers out when we seem to be relying too heavily on our (usually privileged) positions and assumptions. When the story of applied behavioral science is told as a too-small narrative about individuals, please point up to larger systems and structures and remind us that the world we are trying to understand is much bigger than its individual players.

13 CONCLUSION

> Don't get me wrong, I do
> like the flag, how it undulates in the wind
> like water, elemental, and best when it's humbled
> . . .
> when it flickers, when it folds up so perfectly
> you can keep it until it's needed, until you can
> love it again, until the song in your mouth feels
> like sustenance . . .
> . . .
> that song that's our birthright,
> that's sung in silence when it's too hard to go on,
> that sounds like someone's rough fingers weaving
> into another's, that sounds like a match being lit
> in an endless cave, the song that says my bones
> are your bones, and your bones are my bones,
> and isn't that enough?
> —EXCERPT FROM "A NEW NATIONAL ANTHEM," BY ADA LIMÓN

The writer and science communicator Natalia Reagan describes science as a verb, and we agree with that. We want applied behavioral science to be an active, evolving inquiry into the world and ourselves.

Applied behavioral science is still a comparatively new field, which is sometimes evident in our rookie energy, our eagerness to jump in and show our worth by putting points on the board. But after years of proving ourselves, it's been heartening to see the field begin to take stock of our missteps and suggest reforms. It's possible we're ready to cop to what we don't know- which is just in time because only when we name areas of weakness and missteps can we begin to fill in the gaps and push the field forward, along with the pursuit of equity and justice.

We want to lean into this moment, our Epistemic Humility Era. As the scholar Eric Angner explains in The Behavioral Scientist, "epistemic humility is an intellectual virtue. It is grounded in the realization that our knowledge is always provisional and incomplete." He goes on to underline the consequences, "a lack of epistemic humility is a vice—and it can cause massive damage both in our private lives and in public policy."[1]

These stakes motivated us to question our allegiance to common practices. In these chapters, we have explored the limitations and unintended consequences in the way we currently practice applied behavioral science. More importantly, we've offered some critical updates and specific strategies that incorporate principles and approaches for antiracism. The future of applied behavioral science will be made up of work that lifts up and honors the wisdom and lived experiences of communities closest to the challenges we study. To do this, we will need to build authentic and responsible partnerships with BIPOC scholars, community organizations, and universities and work to check the privilege and assumptions of those who have typically held the power in this field.

Our commitment to both applied behavioral science and antiracism is profound and persistent. The critiques we have offered in this book are rooted in deep and genuine love for our colleagues, teachers, our field and its intentions to do good. To paraphrase the poet Amanda Gorman, like America, our field isn't broken, it's simply unfinished. Its next chapters will be written in the work of students, teachers, scholars, funders, NGO teams, and, frankly, anyone who has read this far in this book. What comes next will be the result of individuals pushing our science further by asking questions with humility and fearlessness. The potential of applied behavioral science remains as strong as ever—we hope that this book inspires its readers to take action with us to build its more progressive and inclusive future.

A final note: Ada Limón's poem, "A New National Anthem," intentionally brackets this book, with an excerpt from the first few stanzas opening the preface and an excerpt from the last stanza excerpted in the closing chapter. Early in the poem, Limón points to the controversial original third verse of the national anthem ("and what of the stanzas we never sing, the third that mentions "no refuge could save the hireling and the slave") which was quietly removed from the song we all sing today. Key's original third verse celebrated the death of the freed American slaves who fought alongside the British against the Americans in 1812.[2]

Limón acknowledges these problematic lines and wonders if "every song of this country has an unsung third stanza, something brutal snaking underneath." She wants us to listen—not only to the words on the surface but the ideas hidden beneath them. And in the final lines, the poem asks us to remember, almost reimagine, what is beautiful and radical about America—the aspiration to be liberated, together.

Simply, the poem is both critical and loving. When Limón wrote the poem and submitted it, she said this is the poem "that will make sure that I'm never the poet laureate of the United States."[3] But soon after she was nominated to be the twenty-fourth poet laureate of the United States. When the Librarian of Congress called to tell her she would be poet laureate, she was also asked to read this poem at the ceremony. Calling out injustice is not always rewarded in this way. But when it is, it's worth celebrating. We can and should be critical and loving when it comes to things we cherish, including our science and our field. The risk we take emanates from love.

Acknowledgments

CRYSTAL AND MINDY THANK

We want to thank those who read early versions and made this book far more readable: Nils Mueller, Kelly Bidwell, Todd Rogers, and Syon Bhanot. A special thanks to Dominic Muren for his feedback and his help improving the behavioral map and process images. Kassie Brabaw provided valuable expertise in our editing process.

Early in the process, Jade Chang and Janet Goldstein gave us warm encouragement and pointed the way forward. Michael Hallsworth gave us helpful advice on writing. As we dove into the research, Tara Woodruff was a hardworking and valuable research assistant. Gordon Kraft-Todd added essential insights.

We are grateful to the institutions and people inside them who supported us. At the MIT Press, Bob Prior, our first editor, reached out to us the same day our article in the *Behavioral Scientist* was published because he believed it could be a book. He made us believe that he might be right. Our wonderful editor Matthew Browne has been a skillful and patient partner. At the *Behavioral Scientist*, Dave Nussbaum and Elizabeth Weingarten provided additional support. Access to the University of Washington's beautiful Whiteley Center was a gift of quiet. Ideas need space to flourish. This is especially true for working mothers. We will always be deeply thankful for the time we spent there. At Princeton University, our interest in the field was sparked by the visionary Daniel Kahneman, who passed away on March 27, 2024, just as we were working on final edits of this book. We are deeply grateful for his scholarship. We will miss him, but his work and example will continue to guide us.

We particularly relied on the insights of these scholars and researchers: Ibram X. Kendi, NiCole T. Buchanan (and her colleagues), Nick Chater, George Lowenstein, and especially Ta-Nehisi Coates for both his ideas and beautiful writing. A few people agreed to be interviewed in detail about their work. We are grateful to Dr. Marie Bernard (NIH), Dr. Brittany C. Murray (Davidson College), and Kreg Steven Brown (Washington Center for Equitable Growth). Jennifer Cassidy-Gilbert and Amanda Roose provided access to the skin color card from the National Longitudinal Survey of Youth and the quickest response to an email request we've ever experienced.

Finally, drinks were required throughout this process. We want to thank and toast The Top of the Town Lounge and especially Jeff, who made us feel at home and gave us the respite, laughs, and old-fashioneds that we needed to get back to work.

CRYSTAL THANKS

It feels cliché, but it truly is so hard to acknowledge everyone who has supported me throughout my personal and professional life over the decades. I have tried my best in this space, and I hope that all of my family, friends, and colleagues know how truly lucky I feel.

The Evans School of Public Policy and Governance at the University of Washington has been my academic home for the last fifteen years. My students, faculty, and staff colleagues have challenged me in countless ways—I have grown immensely, thanks to this community. Particular gratitude is due to Jodi Sandfort, Scott Allard, Mary Kay Gugerty, and Heather Hill. Thank you for helping me realize that this was *not* a crazy idea—and for providing the resources and mentorship necessary for me to take this on during an already full season of my academic and personal life. Grant Blume and Ines Jurcevic have been trusted intellectual partners who have also shaped so much of my work in the last several years. You've each taught me so much, and I've been so fortunate to enjoy your friendship and collaboration. The Evans School BAP discussion group helped nurture this idea in its infancy.

That community continues to be an incredible space for support and inspiration. And the amazing GPLunch crew has provided hours of guidance and laughs since my earliest days at the University of Washington. Thank you to Anitra, Becky, Carole, Janneke, Jessica, Kate, and Sapna for being an ever-present safe space and outlet for hard conversations.

Outside of work, I've also been blessed with a fantastic community that has filled my cup when I've needed it most. Enormous thanks to Elan, Margaret, Robin, and Vickie. Because of each of you, I've been able to maintain the physical, mental, and emotional health necessary to do this work. My fantastic book club is a group of women that have inspired me for over a decade. Thank you to Claire, Erin, Jeannie, Rhonda, Shannon, Sharon, and Soni.

Adrienne Russell and John Tomasic blurred the line between the personal and professional in all of the best ways. Your insightful guidance and excellent company helped me weather a pandemic as both a parent and an academic—I can't imagine a better set of neighbors. Ian Mosher and Amarinthia Torres were the core of our pandemic pod and provided valuable support when this idea was in its infancy. Kate Conover, S.J. Crasnow, Martha Galvez, Becky George, Efrain Gutierrez, and Hana Shepherd: in your own way, you have each helped me to find the confidence I've needed to be myself in an increasingly difficult world. I look up to and remain inspired by you, and I'm eternally grateful for your love and wisdom.

There truly aren't words to thank those who have been with me the longest. The pride of my family never fades, and their love and support boosts me every day. Extra special thanks to Mom, Dad, Cyndy, and Grandma—thank you for always believing in me and never even hinting that there might be a limit to what I can accomplish.

And finally, there's no adequate way to thank a partner as exceptional as mine. To Dominic Muren, I truly can't express what your constant love and support have meant. None of my successes have come without you playing a significant role. And to Noah, Carter, and Simone: thank you for being the reason that I try, every single day, to be the best possible version of myself. My ultimate hope is that this book plays a small part in creating the world that you deserve to inherit. You are my forever "why"—and I can't imagine it any other way.

MINDY THANKS

There would be no book if not for Bob Prior. You thought racism and justice were something the MIT Press should talk about, and I'm so grateful for that.

This work and my professional (and personal) life would not exist without John Templeton. You embodied the ideas of antiracism before it was a thing. A visionary gave you keys to the gates of Princeton's MPA program, and you used them to unlock doors to students of color, activists, rebellious intellectuals, Amons, and others who might otherwise have been kept out. For your kindness, encouragement, and faith in me, I am forever grateful.

I owe a huge debt to the writers in my life who I'm lucky enough to count as my closest friends: Jade Chang and Michelle Boorstein, thanks for reassuring me that writing is, in fact, *so* hard. And that whining, procrastinating, and snacks are therefore always allowed. Summer Pierre for reminding me that writing is also a privilege to be enjoyed. Paul Hirsch for showing me what perseverance and great writing look like and for being reliably hilarious ("you eat oat bran in the light").

A few friends provided very early support for which I'm deeply grateful. Andres Henriquez for being an early cheerleader, cracking me up and being our Tío. Tom Bollyky for early, frank advice about both the sacrifice and immense gratification of turning thoughts into words.

Two institutions supported me and this work. Princeton University's School of Public and International Affairs was a beautiful intellectual and spiritual home that sparked my love of behavioral science. I am especially grateful to my teacher and friend Emily Pronin for her early encouragement. The World Resources Institute gave me the flexibility to work on this book and provided an example of an organization striving toward racial justice. I'm especially grateful to Ani Dasgupta and Craig Hanson for their support and to Helen Mountford, whose leadership sets the high-water mark for us all.

To my family: Mom, Marc, Carie, Jack, Ella, Ryan, and Ava. And Jenny for showing me what goodness and grace look like. T.T. Gloria for surviving despite everything and for sharing stories of the family with me.

Carving out time to write a book was only possible because of my partner, Nils. Thank you for carrying more over the last year, for reading early pages with a pencil in hand and a heartwarming amount of care—about me, my ideas, and punctuation. To Oli and Lula for everything you are, and for writing on my office white board, "you can do it, mom!" Because of you both, I did.

Most of all, to, for, because of, and in memory of Victor Luis Hernandez and Delia Visbal Hernandez. To paraphrase the poet, Toi Derricotte, What was done made me. Only they can know who loved best. For whom I have done good.

Appendix: Resources

I. GENERAL RESOURCES

Books

- Ibram X. Kendi, *How to Be an Antiracist* (New York: Random House, 2019).
- Ibram X. Kendi, *Stamped from the Beginning: The Definitive History of Racist Ideas in America* (New York: Bold Type Books, 2017).
- Ijeoma Oluo, *So You Want to Talk about Race* (New York: Seal Press, 2018).
- Robin DiAngelo, *White Fragility: Why It's So Hard for White People to Talk about Racism* (Boston, MA: Beacon Press, 2018).
- Beverly D. Tatum, *Why Are All the Black Kids Sitting Together in the Cafeteria?: And Other Conversations about Race* (New York: Basic Books, 2017).
- Lee Ross and Richard E. Nisbett. *The Person and the Situation: Perspectives of Social Psychology* (London: Pinter & Martin, 2011).

Academic Articles and Projects

- NiCole T. Buchanan, Marisol Perez, Mitchell J. Prinstein, and Idia B. Thurston, "Upending Racism in Psychological Science: Strategies to Change How Science Is Conducted, Reported, Reviewed, and Disseminated," *American Psychologist* 76 (2021): 1097–1112, https://doi.org/10.1037/amp0000905.
- The University of Washington's Participatory Action Transportation for Health in South Seattle (PATHSS) project.

- John A. Garcia, "The Race Project: Researching Race in the Social Sciences Researchers, Measures, and Scope of Studies," *Journal of Race, Ethnicity, and Politics* 2 no. 2 (2017): 300–346, https://doi.org/10.1017/rep.2017.15.
- Resources for disrupting white-centered research practices:
  - Bou Zeineddine et al., "'Some Uninteresting Data from a Faraway Country': Inequity and Coloniality in International Social Psychological Publication," *Journal of Social Issues* 78, no. 2 (2021): 320–345.
  - Alison Ledgerwood et al., "Methods for Advancing an Open, Replicable, and Inclusive Science of Social Cognition," in *Oxford Handbook of Social Cognition*, ed. Kurt Hugenberg, K. Johnson, and Donal E. Carlston (New York: Oxford University Press, in press).
  - Alison Ledgerwood et al. "The Pandemic as a Portal: Reimagining Psychological Science as Truly Open and Inclusive," *Perspectives on Psychological Science* 17, no. 4 (2022): 937–959, https://doi.org/10.1177/17456916211036654.
  - Jessica D. Remedios, "Psychology Must Grapple with Whiteness," *Nature Reviews Psychology* 1 (2022): 125–126, https://doi.org/10.1038/s44159-022-00024-4.

Other Materials

- Economic Policy Institute's Program on Race, Ethnicity, and the Economy
- Washington Center for Equitable Growth—race and ethnicity work.
- Work by Darrick Hamilton and William Darity Jr.
- The Untokening convening and the "Principles of Mobility Justice."
- *Arrested Mobility*, a podcast hosted by Charles Brown (founder and CEO of Equitable Cities, a transportation consulting firm).
- George Mason University InfoGuides: Finding Diverse Voices in Academic Research

II. CHAPTER-SPECIFIC RESOURCES

Introduction

- The 2021 executive order, "Advancing Racial Equity and Support for Underserved Communities through the Federal Government."
- The 2023 executive order, "Further Advancing Racial Equity and Support for Underserved Communities through the Federal Government" (the updated order).
- Martin Luther King Jr., "The Role of the Behavioral Scientist in the Civil Rights Movement," *The American Psychologist* 23, no. 3 (1968): 180–186, https://doi.org/10.1037/h0025715.
- Isabel Wilkerson, *Caste: The Origins of Our Discontents* (New York: Random House, 2020).
- Isabel Wilkerson, "America's Enduring Caste System," *New York Times Magazine*, July 1, 2020, https://www.nytimes.com/2020/07/01/magazine/isabel-wilkerson-caste.html.
- The Reproductive Health Impact: The Collaborative for Equity and Justice organization.

Chapter 1: Applied Behavioral Science

- Frameworks for the application of behavioral insights:
  - EAST: Easy, Attractive, Social, and Timely (from the BIT).
  - SIMPLER (from MDRC and BIAS Project).

Chapter 2: What's at Stake and What's Possible

- Keith Wailoo, *Pushing Cool: Big Tobacco, Racial Marketing, and the Untold Story of the Menthol Cigarette* (Chicago: University of Chicago Press, 2021).
- Brookings Institution's Evidence Speaks series.
- Arnett, Autumn, *Let's Stop Calling it an Achievement Gap: How Public Education in the United States Maintains Disparate Educational Experiences for Students of Color . . . on Access, Equity, and Achievement* (Charlotte, NC: Information Age Publishing, 2019).

Chapter 3: Why We Look Away, and What's Possible When We Don't

- The NIH's Community-Based Participatory Research Program: https://www.nimhd.nih.gov/programs/extramural/community-based-participatory.html#program-description.

Chapter 6: Prepare Your Workplace

- Lang, Angela. "Serving, Organizing, and Empowering Communities of Color: Best Practices for Aligning Research, Advocacy, and Activism." Washington, D.C.: Economic Policy Institute, 2022. https://www.epi.org/publication/serving-organizing-and-empowering-communities-of-color-best-practices-for-aligning-research-advocacy-and-activism/
- Beverly D. Tatum, *Why Are All the Black Kids Sitting Together in the Cafeteria?: And Other Conversations about Race* (New York: Basic Books, 2017).
- McIntosh, Peggy, "White Privilege and Male Privilege: A Personal Account of Coming To See Correspondences through Work in Women's Studies," Working Paper 189. Wellesley, MA: Wellesley College Center for Research on Women (1988). https://psychology.umbc.edu/wp-content/uploads/sites/57/2016/10/White-Privilege_McIntosh-1989.pdf.
- American Medical Association, "Organizational Strategic Plan to Embed Racial Justice and Advance Health Equity," 2021, https://www.ama-assn.org/system/files/ama-equity-strategic-plan.pdf.

Chapter 7: Codefine

- Racial equity toolkit resources from GARE: https://www.racialequityalliance.org/tools-resources/.

Chapter 8: Codiscover

- A guide to the PRA: https://pra.digital.gov/
- Alice McIntyre, *Participatory Action Research* (Thousand Oaks, CA: SAGE Publications, 2007).

Chapter 9: Codesign

- Akee, Randall, "Racial Equity in U.S. Data Collection Improves the Accuracy of Research, Policy Evaluation, and Subsequent Policymaking," Washington,

DC: Center for Equitable Growth, (2021). https://equitablegrowth.org/racial-equity-in-u-s-data-collection-improves-the-accuracy-of-research-policy-evaluation-and-subsequent-policymaking/.
- National Asset Scorecard, created in collaboration with faculty and researchers from the Samuel DuBois Cook Center on Social Equity.
- "Racial and Ethnic Disparities in the United States: An Interactive Chartbook." Washington D.C.: Economic Policy Institute, 2022. https://www.epi.org/publication/disparities-chartbook/.
- IDEO.org resources: https://www.designkit.org/methods.html.
- Katy B. Kozhimannil, "Doula Care, Birth Outcomes, and Costs among Medicaid Beneficiaries," *American Journal of Public Health* 103, no. 4 (2013): e113–e121, https://www.ncbi.nlm.nih.gov/pmc/articles/PMC3617571/.

Chapter 10: Implement and Interpret

- Economic Policy Institute. "Race and Ethnicity in Empirical Analysis: How Should We Interpret the Race Variable?" Washington, DC: Economic Policy Institute, 2023. https://www.federalreserve.gov/econres/notes/feds-notes/improving-the-measurement-of-racial-and-ethnic-disparities-in-the-survey-of-consumer-finances-20210621.html
- Steven Brown, Graham MacDonald, and Claire Bowen, "How the Federal Government Can Use Data to Make the Most of the Executive Order on Racial Equity," *Urban Wire* (blog), January 29, 2021, https://www.urban.org/urban-wire/how-federal-government-can-use-data-make-most-executive-order-racial-equity.
- Austin Clemens and Michael Garvey, "Structural Racism and the Coronavirus Recession Highlight Why More and Better US Data Need to Be Widely Disaggregated by Race and Ethnicity," Equitable Growth, September 24, 2020, https://equitablegrowth.org/structural-racism-and-the-coronavirus-recession-highlight-why-more-and-better-u-s-data-need-to-be-widely-disaggregated-by-race-and-ethnicity/.
- Allen Fremont, Joel S. Weissman, Emily Hoch, and Marc N. Elliott, "When Race/Ethnicity Data Are Lacking: Using Advanced Indirect Estimation Methods to Measure Disparities," *RAND Health Quarterly*

- 6, no. 1, https://www.rand.org/pubs/periodicals/health-quarterly/issues/v6/n1/16.html.
- A 2008 MSNBC "Conversation About Race" video shares an updated version of the classic Doll Test with Black and Latino children: https://www.youtube.com/watch?v=tkpUyB2xgTM.
- Skin tone measure from the National Longitudinal Survey of Youth and the skin color card for NLSY97: https://nlsinfo.org/sites/default/files/attachments/140114/skin%20color%20card%20for%20NLSY97.pdf.
- Greta R. Bauer and Ayden I. Scheim, "Methods for Analytic Intercategorical Intersectionality in Quantitative Research: Discrimination as a Mediator of Health Inequalities," *Social Science and Medicine* 226: 236–245, https://www.sciencedirect.com/science/article/pii/S0277953618306889#sec4.
- Assistant Secretary for Planning and Evaluation, "Advancing Equity by Incorporating Intersectionality in Research and Analysis," September 2022, https://aspe.hhs.gov/sites/default/files/documents/80123172bbe4458a06259535dc3fcfc3/Intresectionality-Resrch-Anlysis.pdf.
- Mary K. Gugerty and Dean Karlan, *The Goldilocks Challenge: Right-Fit Evidence for the Social Sector* (Oxford: Oxford University Press, 2018).

Chapter 11: Share, Adapt, and Scale

- K. Steven Brown, Kilolo Kijakazi, Charmaine Runes, and Margery A. Turner, "Confronting Structural Racism in Research and Policy Analysis: Charting a Course for Policy Research Institutions," Urban Institute, February 2019, https://www.urban.org/research/publication/confronting-structural-racism-research-and-policy-analysis.
- Chautard, Alice, "Inclusive Conferences? We Can and Must Do Better–Here's How." United Kingdom: London School of Economics Impact of Social Sciences blog, 2019. https://blogs.lse.ac.uk/impactofsocialsciences/2019/06/06/inclusive-conferences-we-can-and-must-do-better-heres-how/.
- Brittany Murray, Elsa Falkenburger, and Priya Saxena, "Data Walks: An Innovative Way to Share Data with Communities," Urban Institute, November 10, 2015, https://www.urban.org/research/publication/data-walks-innovative-way-share-data-communities.

- Jonathan Schwabish and Alice Fend, "Do No Harm Guide: Applying Equity Awareness in Data Visualization," Urban Institute, June 9, 2021. https://www.urban.org/sites/default/files/publication/104296/do-no-harm-guide.pdf.
- NiCole T. Buchanan, Marisol Perez, Mitchell J. Prinstein, and Idia B. Thurston, "Upending Racism in Psychological Science: Strategies to Change How Science Is Conducted, Reported, Reviewed, and Disseminated," *American Psychologist* 76 (2021): 1097–1112, https://doi.org/10.1037/amp0000905.

Chapter 12: Action Agenda
- American Psychological Association, "American Psychological Foundation: MFP Fund for Racial and Ethnic Diversity," last updated November 2023, https://www.apa.org/apf/funding/mfp.
- Steven Brown, Graham MacDonald, and Claire Bowen, "How the Federal Government Can Use Data to Make the Most of the Executive Order on Racial Equity," *Urban Wire* (blog), January 29, 2021, https://www.urban.org/urban-wire/how-federal-government-can-use-data-make-most-executive-order-racial-equity.

Notes

PREFACE

1. Crystal C. Hall and Mindy Hernandez, "Breaking the Silence: Can Behavioral Science Confront Structural Racism?" *Behavioral Scientist*, June 21, 2021, https://behavioralscientist.org/breaking-the-silence-can-behavioral-science-confront-structural-racism/.

2. Nambi Ndugga, Latoya Hill, and Samantha Artiga, "COVID-19 Cases and Deaths, Vaccinations, and Treatments by Race/Ethnicity as of Fall 2022," KFF (blog), November 17, 2022, https://www.kff.org/racial-equity-and-health-policy/issue-brief/covid-19-cases-and-deaths-vaccinations-and-treatments-by-race-ethnicity-as-of-fall-2022.

3. US Census Bureau, "Long COVID-19 Symptoms Reported," May 23, 2023. https://www.census.gov/library/stories/2023/05/long-covid-19-symptoms-reported.html.

4. National Academies of Sciences, Engineering, and Medicine, "More Investment and Attention Needed to Address Pandemic-Related Harms on Children and Families in Marginalized Communities," March 16, 2023, https://www.nationalacademies.org/news/2023/03/more-investment-and-attention-needed-to-address-pandemic-related-harms-on-children-and-families-in-marginalized-communities.

5. Christopher W. Tessum et al., "Inequity in Consumption of Goods and Services Adds to Racial–Ethnic Disparities in Air Pollution Exposure," *Proceedings of the National Academy of Sciences* 116, no. 13 (2019): 6001–6006, https://doi.org/10.1073/pnas.1818859116; Solomon Hsiang et al., "Estimating Economic Damage from Climate Change in the United States," *Science* 356, no. 6345 (2017): 1362–1369, https://doi.org/10.1126/science.aal4369.

DEFINITIONS

1. According to Sunstein and Thaler, Econs are models of perfectly rational beings that process all available information and never make decisions based on irrelevant emotional states. They maximize their expected utility, exhibit willpower, never procrastinate, and are not influenced by irrelevant factors or trade-offs between present and future.

2. We borrow these definitions from the scholar Ibram X. Kendi.

INTRODUCTION

1. "Executive Order—Using Behavioral Science Insights to Better Serve the American People," WhiteHouse.gov, September 15, 2015, https://obamawhitehouse.archives.gov/the-press-office/2015/09/15/executive-order-using-behavioral-science-insights-better-serve-american.

2. In this book we use the imperfect term Latino rather than the newer, alternative label, Latinx. Latinx is a well-meaning attempt to create a gender-inclusive term, but we don't use it because it's not embraced by the community it describes: only 3 percent of US Latinos use the term. It's an anglicization of a Spanish word that doesn't make sense in Spanish.

3. Hyungjo Hur et al., "Recent Trends in the US Behavioral and Social Sciences Research (BSSR) Workforce," *PLOS One* 12, no. 2 (2017): e0170887, https://doi.org/10.1371/journal.pone.0170887.

4. Colorism and racism are deeply connected to colonialism, affecting communities of color worldwide. Our field would benefit from in-depth examinations of how applied behavioral science has avoided addressing these underlying issues in our global endeavors, especially by people from communities of color outside the United States. In this book, we narrow our focus on impacts and pathways forward specifically for the United States.

5. U.S. Department of the Treasury. "Racial Differences in Economic Security: Non-Housing Assets," January 10, 2023, https://home.treasury.gov/news/featured-stories/racial-differences-in-economic-security-non-housing-assets; Kim-Eng Ky and Katherine Lim, "The Role of Race in Mortgage Application Denials," Federal Reserve Bank of Minneapolis, January 5, 2022, https://www.minneapolisfed.org/research/community-development-working-papers/the-role-of-race-in-mortgage-application-denials.

6. United States Department of Labor. "Earnings Disparities by Race and Ethnicity," accessed March 20, 2024, http://www.dol.gov/agencies/ofccp/about/data/earnings/race-and-ethnicity.

7. A 2015 Stanford study provided quantitative evidence for Rock's observation and found that Black and Hispanic families effectively need much higher incomes than white families to live in comparably affluent neighborhoods. See Sean F. Reardon, Lindsay Fox, and Joseph Townsend, "Neighborhood Income Composition by Race and Income, 1990–2009," *The Annals of the American Academy of Political and Social Science* 660, no. 660 (2015): 78.

8. Darrick Hamilton and William A. Darity Jr, "The Political Economy of Education, Financial Literacy, and the Racial Wealth Gap," *Review* 99, no. 1 (2017): 59–76, https://doi.org/10.20955/r.2017.59-76; William Darity Jr. et al., "What We Get Wrong about Closing the Racial Wealth Gap," Samuel DuBois Cook Center on Social Equity, April 2018, https://socialequity.duke.edu/research-duke/what-we-get-wrong-about-closing-the-racial-wealth-gap/.

9. We borrow the term "racist blind" from the scholar Yoon K. Pak. See Yoon K. Pak, "'Racist-Blind, Not Color-Blind' by Design: Confronting Systemic Racism in Our Educational Past,

Present, and Future," *History of Education Quarterly* 61, no. 2 (2021): 127–149, https://doi.org/10.1017/heq.2021.5. The term "color silent" comes from Beverly Daniel Tatum, "Why Are All the Black Kids Sitting Together in the Cafeteria?" It refers to the avoidance of discussing race and racism to avoid uncomfortable conversations or being seen as racist. Tatum argues that this approach ultimately perpetuates racism and reinforces racial hierarchies by failing to acknowledge and address systemic inequalities. See Beverly D. Tatum, *Why Are All the Black Kids Sitting Together in the Cafeteria?: And Other Conversations about Race* (New York: Basic Books, 2017).

10. Ibram X. Kendi, *How to Be an Antiracist* (New York: One World, 2019), 18.

11. Nayyirah Waheed, *salt.* (self-published, 2013).

12. Behavioral scientists should also strive to take an intersectional approach. The civil rights leader and scholar Kimberlé Crenshaw introduced the theory of intersectionality, which examines how overlapping social identities (such as race and gender) relate to systems of oppression. In chapter 10, we discuss this concept in more detail.

13. Michael J. Hanmer and Samuel B Novey, "Who Lacked Photo ID in 2020? An Exploration of the American National Election Studies," *Center for Democracy and Civil Engagement*, March 13, 2023. https://www.voteriders.org/wp-content/uploads/2023/04/CDCE_VoteRiders_ANES2020Report_Spring2023.pdf.

14. Jennifer Darrah-Okike, Nathalie Rita, and John R. Logan, "The Suppressive Impacts of Voter Identification Requirements," *Sociological Perspectives* 64, no. 4 (2021): 536–562, https://doi.org/10.1177/0731121420966620; John Kuk, Zoltan Hajnal, and Nazita Lajevardi, "A Disproportionate Burden: Strict Voter Identification Laws and Minority Turnout," *Politics, Groups, and Identities* 10, no. 1 (2022): 126–134, https://doi.org/10.1080/21565503.2020.1773280.

15. "Systemic Racism, a Key Risk Factor for Maternal Death and Illness," National Heart, Lung, and Blood Institute; April 26, 2021, https://www.nhlbi.nih.gov/news/2021/systemic-racism-key-risk-factor-maternal-death-and-illness.

16. National Heart, Lung, and Blood Institute, "Systemic Racism, a Key Risk Factor for Maternal Death and Illness," April 26, 2021, https://www.nhlbi.nih.gov/news/2021/systemic-racism-key-risk-factor-maternal-death-and-illness.

17. In fact, a 2019 study found that across 1,149 articles published in 2015 and 2016 in eleven psychology journals, 73 percent of them never mentioned the race of their participants. Similar data in behavioral studies is not available. See Jasmine M. DeJesus, Maureen A. Callanan, Graciela Solis, and Susan A. Gelman, "Generic Language in Scientific Communication," *Proceedings of the National Academy of Sciences* 116, no. 37 (2019): 18370–18377, https://doi.org/10.1073/pnas.1817706116.

18. Katy B. Kozhimannil, Carrie A. Vogelsang, Rachel R. Hardeman, and Shailendra Prasad, "Disrupting the Pathways of Social Determinants of Health: Doula Support during Pregnancy and Childbirth," *The Journal of the American Board of Family Medicine* 29, no. 3 (2016): 308–317.

19. Lindsay M. Mallick, Marie E. Thoma, and Edmond D. Shenassa, "The Role of Doulas in Respectful Care for Communities of Color and Medicaid Recipients," *Birth: Issues in Perinatal Care* 49, no. 4 (2022): 823–832, https://doi.org/10.1111/birt.12655.

20. Brad N. Greenwood, Rachel R. Hardeman, Laura Huang, and Aaron Sojourner, "Physician-Patient Racial Concordance and Disparities in Birthing Mortality for Newborns," *Proceedings of the National Academy of Sciences of the United States of America* 117, no. 35 (2020): 21194–21200, https://doi.org/10.1073/pnas.1913405117.

21. For example, Katy B. Kozhimannil and colleagues simulated annual cost impacts to state Medicaid programs that might result from a reduction in cesarean delivery rates associated with the reimbursement of birth doula services. Using the reduction in births they documented with a local doula organization, they projected that annual savings might exceed $2.5 million for up to a quarter of all states. See Kozhimannil, Vogelsang, Hardeman, and Prasad, "Disrupting the Pathways of Social Determinants of Health."

22. We paraphrase a favorite quote of President Barack Obama, initially popularized by Martin Luther King, Jr., who paraphrased a sermon by Theodore Parker, an 1850s abolitionist activist. See Mychal Denzel Smith, "The Truth about 'The Arc of the Moral Universe,'" *HuffPost*, January 18, 2018, https://www.huffpost.com/entry/opinion-smith-obama-king_n_5a5903e0e4b04f3c55a252a4.

23. Nick Chater and George Loewenstein, "The I-Frame and the S-Frame: How Focusing on Individual-Level Solutions Has Led Behavioral Public Policy Astray," *Behavioral and Brain Sciences* 46 (2023): e147.

24. Frank Pasquale, "Why 'Nudges' Hardly Help," *The Atlantic*, December 4, 2015, https://www.theatlantic.com/business/archive/2015/12/nudges-effectiveness/418749/.

25. It's worth noting that this thoughtful and important paper does not once mention racism and only gives a brief mention of equity. However, many published commentaries on this article have engaged those topics more deeply.

26. "Fact Sheet: Proposed Product Standards to Prohibit Menthol as a Characterizing Flavor in Cigarettes and All Characterizing Flavors (Other than Tobacco) in Cigars." *United States Food and Drug Administration*, n.d. https://www.fda.gov/media/158015/download?attachment.

27. Today, nearly nine in ten Black smokers prefer menthol cigarettes, which are easier to smoke and harder to quit. It's not an accident that tobacco-related diseases are still the number one cause of death in the African American community. For more, see our case study, "Big Tobacco's Big (and Deadly) Success," in chapter 2.

28. "Executive Order on Advancing Racial Equity and Support for Underserved Communities through the Federal Government," The White House, January 20, 2021, https://www.whitehouse.gov/briefing-room/presidential-actions/2021/01/20/executive-order-advancing-racial-equity-and-support-for-underserved-communities-through-the-federal-government/; "Executive Order on Further Advancing Racial Equity and Support for

Underserved Communities through the Federal Government," The White House, February 16, 2023, https://www.whitehouse.gov/briefing-room/presidential-actions/2023/02/16/executive-order-on-further-advancing-racial-equity-and-support-for-underserved-communities-through-the-federal-government/.

29. Martin Luther King Jr., "The Role of the Behavioral Scientist in the Civil Rights Movement," *The American Psychologist* 23, no. 3 (1968): 180–186, https://doi.org/10.1037/h0025715.

30. "Commissioner Daniel Werfel Letter on Audit Selection," Internal Revenue Service, May 15, 2023, https://www.irs.gov/pub/newsroom/werfel-letter-on-audit-selection.pdf.

31. Katherine Miller, "IRS Disproportionately Audits Black Taxpayers," January 31, 2023, https://hai.stanford.edu/news/irs-disproportionately-audits-black-taxpayers.

32. Jonathan Franklin, "IRS Chief Says Agency Is 'Deeply Concerned' by Higher Audit Rates for Black Taxpayers," *NPR*, May 16, 2023, https://www.npr.org/2023/05/16/1176441745/irs-audits-black-taxpayers.

CHAPTER 1

1. Maria G. Hoffman, Mark A. Klee, and Briana Sullivan, "New Data Reveal Inequality in Retirement Account Ownership," Census.gov., August 31, 2022, https://www.census.gov/library/stories/2022/08/who-has-retirement-accounts.html.

2. Capitalize, "The True Cost of Forgotten 401(k) Accounts (2023)," June 13, 2023, https://www.hicapitalize.com/resources/the-true-cost-of-forgotten-401ks/.

3. This data point definitely did not come up when one of us had to google "how to find lost 401(k)" because she had, in fact, lost track of a 401(k) account.

4. Lincoln Quillian, Devah Pager, Ole Hexel, and Arnfinn H. Midtbøen, "Meta-Analysis of Field Experiments Shows No Change in Racial Discrimination in Hiring over Time," *Proceedings of the National Academy of Sciences* 114, no. 41 (2017): 10870–10875.

5. Anthony Nardone, Joey Chiang, and Jason Corburn, "Historic Redlining and Urban Health Today in US Cities," *Environmental Justice* 13, no. 4 (2020): 109–119.

6. In contrast, stratification economics points out that this discriminatory behavior is driven by a rational notion that groups view themselves as being in competition with one another. And in America, structural forces limiting opportunities for Black Americans were set up by white Americans in the rational (if discriminatory) pursuit to preserve their economic dominance. See William A. Darity, Jr., "Position and Possessions: Stratification Economics and Intergroup Inequality," *Journal of Economic Literature* 60, no. 2 (2022): 400–426.

7. Herbert A. Simon, "Bounded Rationality," in *Utility and Probability*, edited by John Eatwell, Murray Milgate, and Peter Newman (London: Palgrave Macmillan UK, 1990), 15–18.

8. Sendhil Mullainathan and Eldar Shafir describe this issue at length in their 2013 book. See Sendhil Mullainathan and Eldar Shafir, *Scarcity: Why Having Too Little Means So Much* (New York: Macmillan, 2013).

9. These terms were originally coined by psychologists Keith Stanovich and Richard West. See Keith E. Stanovich and Richard F. West, "Individual Differences in Reasoning: Implications for the Rationality Debate?," *Behavioral and Brain Sciences* 23, no. 5 (2020): 645–665, https://doi.org/10.1017/s0140525x00003435.

10. See also EAST and SIMPLER, two popular frameworks that have been used to describe the most common applications of behavioral insights. See the resources section of this book for more information on these frameworks.

11. Sara E. Gorman and Jack M. Gorman, "Avoidance of Complexity," in *Denying to the Grave: Why We Ignore the Science That Will Save Us*, ed. Sara E. Gorman and Jack M. Gorman (Oxford: Oxford University Press, 2021).

12. Julie Rovner, "Problems Plague Rollout of New Medicare Drug Plan," *NPR*, January 11, 2006, https://www.npr.org/templates/story/story.php?storyId=5148817.

13. Christine Lagorio, "MySpace Pulls Ahead in Page View Race," July 12, 2006, https://www.cbsnews.com/news/myspace-pulls-ahead-in-page-view-race/.

14. Eric P. Bettinger, Bridget T. Long, Philip Oreopoulos, and Lisa Sanbonmatsu, "The Role of Application Assistance and Information in College Decisions: Results from the H&R Block FAFSA Experiment," *Quarterly Journal of Economics* 127, no. 3 (2012): 1205–1242, https://doi.org/10.1093/qje/qjs017.

15. Ted O'Donoghue and Matthew Rabin, "Doing It Now or Later," *American Economic Review* 89, no. 1 (1999): 103–124, https://doi.org/10.1257/aer.89.1.103; Ted O'Donoghue and Matthew Rabin, "Present Bias: Lessons Learned and to Be Learned," *American Economic Review* 105, no. 5 (2015): 273–279, https://doi.org/10.1257/aer.p20151085.

16. Robert Cialdini, "Don't Throw in the Towel: Use Social Influence Research," *APS Observer*, April 24, 2005, https://www.psychologicalscience.org/observer/dont-throw-in-the-towel-use-social-influence-research.

17. Wesley P. Schultz, Azar M. Khazian, and Adam C. Zaleski, "Using Normative Social Influence to Promote Conservation among Hotel Guests," *Social Influence* 3, no. 1 (2008): 4–23, https://doi.org/10.1080/15534510701755614.

18. The social psychologist Robert Cialdini is an expert in this space. The field studies he has conducted with his collaborators have provided evidence of these effects in many domains. For more resources, see his website: www.influenceatwork.com/.

19. Howard Leventhal and William Mace, "The Effect of Laughter on Evaluation of a Slapstick Movie," *Journal of Personality* 38, no. 1 (1970): 16–30.

20. Markus Giesler and Ela Veresiu, "Creating the Responsible Consumer: Moralistic Governance Regimes and Consumer Subjectivity," *Journal of Consumer Research* 41, no. 3 (2014): 840–857, https://doi.org/10.1086/677842.

21. Michael Hallsworth, "Misconceptions about the Practice of Behavioral Public Policy" (working paper, January 2023), https://doi.org/10.2139/ssrn.4328659.

22. See Tversky and Kahneman for early research that popularized this behavioral science approach: Amos Tversky and Daniel Kahneman, "Rational Choice and the Framing of Decisions," *Decision Making: Descriptive, Normative, and Prescriptive Interactions* (1988): 167–192.

23. John M. Darley and C. Daniel Batson, "'From Jerusalem to Jericho': A Study of Situational and Dispositional Variables in Helping Behavior," *Journal of Personality and Social Psychology* 27 (1973): 100–108, https://doi.org/10.1037/h0034449.

24. For example, simplification can be a way to make some processes easier to understand and attractive, but this may not always be true. For example, a recent study led by Elizabeth Linos showed that formal communications from governments were viewed as more trustworthy and competent than those designed to be informal. The researchers believed that people infer credibility and importance from more formal language. In this case, the context clearly matters. See Elizabeth Linos et al., "The Formality Effect" (working paper, January 2023), https://doi.org/10.2139/ssrn.4344196.

25. Elizabeth Rusch, "Maria Anna Mozart: The Family's First Prodigy," *Smithsonian Magazine*, March 27, 2011, https://www.smithsonianmag.com/arts-culture/maria-anna-mozart-the-familys-first-prodigy-1259016/.

26. "Breaking Free of Stereotype Threat with Claude Steele (Transcript)," *ReThinking with Adam Grant* (podcast), accessed March 20, 2024, https://www.ted.com/podcasts/breaking-free-of-stereotype-threat-claude-steele-transcript.

27. Claude M. Steele and Joshua Aronson, "Stereotype Threat and the Intellectual Test Performance of African Americans," *Journal of Personality and Social Psychology* 69, no. 5 (1995): 797.

28. Jonathan Schulz, Duman Bahrami-Rad, Jonathan Beauchamp, and Joseph Henrich, "The Origins of WEIRD Psychology" (working paper June 2018), https://doi.org/10.2139/ssrn.3201031.

29. Joseph Henrich, Steven J. Heine, and Ara Norenzayan, "Most People Are Not WEIRD," *Nature* 466, no. 7302 (2010): 29–29, https://doi.org/10.1038/466029a.

30. Hyungjo Hur et al., "Recent Trends in the US Behavioral and Social Sciences Research (BSSR) Workforce," *PLOS One* 12, no. 2 (2017), https://doi.org/10.1371/journal.pone.0170887.

CHAPTER 2

1. Richard H. Thaler and Shlomo Benartzi, "Save More Tomorrow™: Using Behavioral Economics to Increase Employee Saving," *Journal of Political Economy* 112, no. S1 (2004): S164–S187, https://doi.org/10.1086/380085.

2. John Beshears et al., "Public Policy and Saving for Retirement: The Autosave Features of the Pension Protection Act of 2006," in *Better Living through Economics*, edited by John J. Siegfried (Cambridge, MA: Harvard University Press, 2010), 274–296.

3. Hunt Allcott, "Social Norms and Energy Conservation," *Journal of Public Economics* 95, no. 9 (2011): 1082–1095, https://doi.org/10.1016/j.jpubeco.2011.03.003.

4. Hunt Allcott and Todd Rogers, "The Short-Run and Long-Run Effects of Behavioral Interventions: Experimental Evidence from Energy Conservation," *American Economic Review* 104, no. 10 (2014): 3003–3037, https://doi.org/10.1257/aer.104.10.3003.

5. It's worth noting that these results, while incredibly impressive and important, were slightly more complicated than they may appear. The initial work showed what researchers call a "boomerang effect," where relatively low-usage individuals increase their consumption when receiving the usage behavior of others. This effect seems to be eliminated by including energy conservation information in addition to "injunctive" norm messaging (information about what is moral or right).

6. For more information and a history, see http://www.bi.team.

7. "Executive Order—Using Behavioral Science Insights to Better Serve the American People," The White House, September 15, 2015, https://obamawhitehouse.archives.gov/the-press-office/2015/09/15/executive-order-using-behavioral-science-insights-better-serve-american.

8. Shlomo Benartzi et al., "Should Governments Invest More in Nudging?" *Psychological Science* 28, no. 8 (2017): 1041–1055, https://doi.org/10.1177/0956797617702501.

9. Organisation for Economic Co-operation and Development, "Behavioural Insights," accessed March 20, 2024, https://www.oecd.org/gov/regulatory-policy/behavioural-insights.htm.

10. For example, DellaVigna and Linos look at 126 RCTs covering twenty-three million individuals, including all interventions from two of the large government nudge units in the United States. They find the average impact of the interventions studied is 1.4 percentage points (an 8.0 percent increase from the comparison). See Stefano DellaVigna and Elizabeth Linos, "RCTs to Scale: Comprehensive Evidence from Two Nudge Units," *Econometrica* 90, no. 1 (2022): 81–116, https://doi.org/10.3982/ECTA18709.

11. Chater and Loewenstein, and more recently Michael Hallsworth. Both have been previously discussed.

12. Very few working in the field were upfront and direct about the limited potential size of the anticipated impacts. Although one prominent report stated that "these types of interventions are not always expected, or intended, to achieve enormous impacts or attain a system overhaul. Instead, they are meant to be responsive to behavioral tendencies and to foster change at relatively low cost and effort." Nadine Dechausay, Caitlin Anzelone, and Leigh Reardon, "The Power of Prompts: Using Behavioral Insights to Encourage People to Participate," *OPRE Report* 75 (2015).

13. VITA sites offer many services beyond savings bonds. Often, they aim to put people in touch with legitimate debt management NGOs, employment agencies, and other social services aimed to help people manage low incomes and spiraling debt. However, most academics at this point were interested in savings, in part because the data was possible to collect and the

behavioral outcome quantifiable, as opposed to getting data on who actually took up a service, which is notoriously difficult.

14. Since these early studies, the field became much more nuanced about how individuals experiencing poverty save.

15. Neil Bhutta et al., "Disparities in Wealth by Race and Ethnicity in the 2019 Survey of Consumer Finances," FEDS Notes, September 28, 2020, https://www.federalreserve.gov/econres/notes/feds-notes/disparities-in-wealth-by-race-and-ethnicity-in-the-2019-survey-of-consumer-finances-20200928.html.

16. As of 2022, American Indian and Alaska Native (AIAN) and Hispanic people had the highest uninsured rates, at 19 percent and 18 percent, respectively. Uninsured rates for Black people were 10 percent, while that of white people were 7 percent. See Samantha Artiga, Latoya Hill, and Anthony Damico Published, "Health Coverage by Race and Ethnicity, 2010–2021," *KFF* (blog), December 20, 2022, https://www.kff.org/racial-equity-and-health-policy/issue-brief/health-coverage-by-race-and-ethnicity/.

17. Darrick Hamilton and William A. Darity Jr., "The Political Economy of Education, Financial Literacy, and the Racial Wealth Gap," *Review* 99, no. 1 (2017): 59–76, https://doi.org/10.20955/r.2017.59-76.

18. The BIAS project was led by MDRC (a prominent social policy research firm), and there have been several projects in this portfolio since the initial research was published in 2017. See Lashawn Richburg-Hayes, Caitlin Anzelone, and Nadine Dechausay, "Nudging Change in Human Services: Final Report of the Behavioral Interventions to Advance Self-Sufficiency (BIAS) Project" (working paper, May 2017), https://papers.ssrn.com/abstract=3007745.

19. Specifically, BIAS focused on three program areas: child support, childcare, and work support.

20. The original SBST website archived can be found at sbst.gov/.

21. Daniel D. Shephard, Crystal C. Hall, and Cait Lamberton, "Increasing Identification of Homeless Students: An Experimental Evaluation of Increased Communication Incorporating Behavioral Insights," *Educational Researcher* 50, no. 4 (2021): 239–248, https://doi.org/10.3102/0013189X20981067.

22. Note that the researchers looked at college attendance, not completion.

23. Darrick Hamilton et al., "Why Black Colleges and Universities Still Matter," *The American Prospect*, November 9, 2015, https://prospect.org/api/content/3178845a-b487-5c47-b131-23fcf4c38510/.

24. Mark Huelsman, "Betrayers of the Dream: How Sleazy For-Profit Colleges Disproportionately Targeted Black Students," *The American Prospect* 26, no. 3 (2015): 9–11.

25. Phillip Levine and Dubravka Ritter, "The Racial Wealth Gap, Financial Aid, and College Access," Brookings Institution, September 27, 2022, https://www.brookings.edu/articles/the-racial-wealth-gap-financial-aid-and-college-access/.

26. Fenaba R. Addo and Xing S. Zhang, "Gender Stratification, Racial Disparities, and Student Debt Trajectories in Young Adulthood" (working paper, November 2022), https://www.stlouisfed.org/-/media/project/frbstl/stlouisfed/files/pdfs/iee/eei/wocstl-stlfed-03-nov-2022.pdf.

27. Eileen Patten, "Racial, Gender Wage Gaps Persist in US despite Some Progress," *Pew Research Center* (blog), 2016, https://www.pewresearch.org/short-reads/2016/07/01/racial-gender-wage-gaps-persist-in-u-s-despite-some-progress/.

28. In reference to private colleges. See Huelsman, "Betrayers of the Dream."

29. In 2016, the six-year graduation rate for first-time, full-time undergraduate students who began their pursuit of a bachelor's degree at a four-year degree-granting institution was 64 percent for white students, 54 percent for Latino students, 40 percent for Black students, and just 39 percent for American Indian/Alaska Native students. See National Center for Education Statistics, "Indicator 23: Postsecondary Graduation Rates," last updated February 2019, https://nces.ed.gov/programs/raceindicators/indicator_red.asp.

30. Judith Scott-Clayton and Jing Li, "Black-White Disparity in Student Loan Debt More than Triples after Graduation," Brookings Institution, October 20, 2016, https://www.brookings.edu/articles/black-white-disparity-in-student-loan-debt-more-than-triples-after-graduation/.

31. Colleen Campbell, "The Forgotten Faces of Student Loan Default," Center for American Progress, October 16, 2018, https://www.americanprogress.org/article/forgotten-faces-student-loan-default/.

32. Jalil B. Mustaffa and Jonathan C.W. Davis, "Jim Crow Debt: How Black Borrowers Experience Student Loans," Education Trust, 2021.

33. The FAFSA program itself does not currently collect demographic information, making collecting this information difficult. However, it will be required when the FAFSA Simplification Act goes into effect in 2024.

34. For an excellent history of how big tobacco targeted Black customers, see Keith Wailoo, *Pushing Cool: Big Tobacco, Racial Marketing, and the Untold Story of the Menthol Cigarette* (Chicago: University of Chicago Press, 2021).

35. Not a single advertisement for a nonmenthol brand ever appeared in the leading African American magazine *Ebony* in its seventy-year existence under its original publisher—and not a single article ever appeared on the leading preventable cause of death among African Americans: cigarette smoking.

36. Charles Brown, J'Lin Rose, and Samuel Kling, "Arrested Mobility: Barriers to Walking, Biking, and e-Scooter Use in Black Communities in the United States," March 2023, https://arrestedmobility.com/wp-content/uploads/2023/03/Arrested-Mobility-Report_web.pdf.

37. In 2020, the FDA finally banned the sale of flavored cigarettes, including menthol.

38. Thomas R. Kirchner et al., "Tobacco Retail Outlet Advertising Practices and Proximity to Schools, Parks and Public Housing Affect Synar Underage Sales Violations in Washington,

DC," *Tobacco Control* 24, no. e1 (2015): e52–e58, https://doi.org/10.1136/tobaccocontrol-2013-051239.

CHAPTER 3

1. The authors of this paper defined a "focus on race" as a paper that directly mentioned the racial identity of participants in the abstract. They also found that the race of a publications' primary editor and board members were indicative of the amount of race-focused research that was published. See Steven O. Roberts et al., "Racial Inequality in Psychological Research: Trends of the Past and Recommendations for the Future," *Perspectives on Psychological Science* 15, no. 6 (2020): 1295–1309.

2. Eden B. King, Derek R. Avery, Mikki R. Hebl, and Jose M. Cortina, "Systematic Subjectivity: How Subtle Biases Infect the Scholarship Review Process," *Journal of Management* 44, no. 3 (2018): 843–853.

3. Kafui Dzirasa, "Revising the A Priori Hypothesis: Systemic Racism Has Penetrated Scientific Funding," *Cell* 183, no. 3 (2020): 576–579, https://doi.org/10.1016/j.cell.2020.09.026.

4. John A. Garcia, "The Race Project: Researching Race in the Social Sciences Researchers, Measures, and Scope of Studies," *Journal of Race, Ethnicity, and Politics* 2, no. 2 (2017): 300–346, https://doi.org/10.1017/rep.2017.15.

5. To be fair, at that point we also wanted very much to move on.

6. Robin DiAngelo, *White Fragility: Why It's So Hard for White People to Talk about Racism* (Boston, MA: Beacon Press, 2018).

7. Traditionally, this gap has been referred to as the "achievement gap," but we join Teach for America and other education organizations in moving toward language that recognizes the systemic reasons for this gap. It is also referred to as an "awarding gap." This stresses the reality that these discrepancies exist due to historical and structural disadvantage rather than to individual performance or ability.

8. Mindy gave the talk as written and left the foundation not long after.

9. Pivot was the primary source for this search as well as the NSF tool, the APA tool, and the list of private foundations provided by the Social Psychology Network. Twenty-three key terms were used—all variations of racism, structural racism, racial equity, and so forth.

10. Defined as using any of our twenty-three key terms, which were variations of "structural racism."

11. Kenneth B. Clark and Mamie K. Clark, "Skin Color as a Factor in Racial Identification of Negro Preschool Children," *Journal of Social Psychology* 11, no. 1 (1940): 159–169, https://doi.org/10.1080/00224545.1940.9918741; Kenneth B. Clark and Mamie K. Clark, "The Development of Consciousness of Self and the Emergence of Racial Identification in Negro Preschool Children," *Journal of Social Psychology* 10, no. 4 (1939): 591–599, https://doi.org/10.1080/00224545.1939.9713394.

12. National Archives, "*Brown v. Board of Education*," August 15, 2016, https://www.archives.gov/education/lessons/brown-v-board.

13. Diane Byrd et al., "A Modern Doll Study: Self Concept," *Race, Gender & Class* 24, no. 1–2 (2017): 186–202.

14. Muzafer Sherif, "Superordinate Goals in the Reduction of Intergroup Conflict," *American Journal of Sociology* 63, no. 4 (1958): 349–356, https://doi.org/10.1086/222258.

15. The father of social psychologist Joshua Aronson, mentioned in chapter 1.

16. Elliot Aronson, *The Jigsaw Classroom* (Thousand Oaks, CA: Sage, 1978).

CHAPTER 4

1. Saugato Datta and Sendhil Mullainathan, "Behavioral Design: A New Approach to Development Policy," *Review of Income and Wealth* 60, no. 1 (2014): 7–35, https://doi.org/10.1111/roiw.12093.

2. Since these early days, ideas42 has added community engagement positions to their staff.

3. NIMHD, "Community-Based Participatory Research Program (CBPR)," accessed March 25, 2024, https://www.nimhd.nih.gov/programs/extramural/community-based-participatory.html.

4. When we mention qualitative research methods, we refer to methods that include, but are not limited to, the following techniques: observations, interviews, and focus groups.

5. We define quantitative research methods as those that include the analysis of administrative data (data that is part of an organization's regular record keeping) or survey data, involving rating scales to describe outcomes or variables or to infer relationships between outcomes or variables.

6. Inspiration for this behavioral map comes from the US Agency for International Development's global health and behavior change work, led by Dr. Elizabeth Fox.

7. RCTs randomly assign similar participants to different groups or conditions. One group receives the intervention being tested, while the other group serves as a control and receives no intervention. Because RCTs are designed to control for factors that could influence the outcome, they allow researchers to make causal inferences about the intervention's effects. Quasi-experimental evaluations may involve groups that are not randomly assigned and/or may lack a control group. These studies can be "hypothesis suggesting" and explore cause-and-effect relationships, but they are not "hypothesis proving." Nonexperimental studies do not involve randomly assigning participants to different groups or conditions. Instead, they typically involve observing and measuring naturally occurring behaviors, attitudes, or other variables. While nonexperimental studies are useful for describing and understanding the relationships between different variables, they do not allow researchers to make causal inferences.

8. Seventy-three percent of psychology papers across eleven journals did not provide any data on the race or ethnicity of their participants.

CHAPTER 5

1. US Census Bureau, "US Census Bureau QuickFacts: District of Columbia," accessed October 30, 2023, https://www.census.gov/quickfacts/fact/table/DC/PST045222.

CHAPTER 6

1. Katherine Schaeffer and Khadijah Edwards, "Black Americans Differ from Other US Adults over whether Individual or Structural Racism Is a Bigger Problem," *Pew Research Center* (blog), November 15, 2022, https://www.pewresearch.org/short-reads/2022/11/15/black-americans-differ-from-other-u-s-adults-over-whether-individual-or-structural-racism-is-a-bigger-problem/.

2. Hasan Kwame Jeffries, "Teaching Hard History," Southern Poverty Law Center, January 31, 2018, https://www.splcenter.org/20180131/teaching-hard-history#summary.

3. Steven O. Roberts and Michael T. Rizzo, "The Psychology of American Racism," *American Psychologist* 76 (2021): 475–487, https://doi.org/10.1037/amp0000642.

4. Simón Rios, "$8: The Complicated Story Behind One of the Most Repeated Statistics about Boston," *WBUR*, July 8, 2021, https://www.wbur.org/news/2021/07/08/greater-boston-black-families-net-worth.

5. Ana P. Muñoz et al., "The Color of Wealth in Boston," Federal Reserve Bank of Boston, March 25, 2015, https://www.bostonfed.org/publications/one-time-pubs/color-of-wealth.aspx.

6. bell hooks, "Yearning: Race, Gender, and Cultural Politics," *Hypatia* 7, no. 2 (1992).

7. Steven O. Roberts et al., "Racial Inequality in Psychological Research: Trends of the Past and Recommendations for the Future," *Perspectives on Psychological Science* 15, no. 6 (2020): 1295–1309.

8. National Institutes of Health, "NIH Stands against Structural Racism in Biomedical Research," February 26, 2021, https://www.nih.gov/about-nih/who-we-are/nih-director/statements/nih-stands-against-structural-racism-biomedical-research.

9. Francis S. Collins et al., "Affirming NIH's Commitment to Addressing Structural Racism in the Biomedical Research Enterprise," *Cell* 184, no. 12 (2021): 3075–3079, https://doi.org/10.1016/j.cell.2021.05.014.

10. Ijeoma Oluo, *So You Want to Talk about Race* (New York: Hachette, 2019), 65.

11. Charles Brown, J'Lin Rose, and Samuel Kling, "Arrested Mobility: Barriers to Walking, Biking, and e-Scooter Use in Black Communities in the United States," March 2023, https://arrestedmobility.com/wp-content/uploads/2023/03/Arrested-Mobility-Report_web.pdf.

12. Evan P. Apfelbaum et al., "Learning (Not) to Talk about Race: When Older Children Underperform in Social Categorization," *Developmental psychology* 44, no. 5 (2008): 1513.

13. Amanda Barroso, "How Often People Talk about Race with Family and Friends Depends on Racial and Ethnic Group, Education, Politics," *Pew Research Center* (blog), June 25, 2019, https://www.pewresearch.org/short-reads/2019/06/25/how-often-people-talk-about-race-with-family-and-friends/.

14. We recommend Robin DiAngelo's "social justice cheat sheet" as a tool for creating shared language within your organization. This is also a critical first step toward engaging in meaningful internal conversations about race and racism.

15. Elizabeth L. Paluck, Roni Porat, Chelsey S. Clark, and Donald P. Green, "Prejudice Reduction: Progress and Challenges," *Annual Review of Psychology* 72 (2021): 533–560.

CHAPTER 7

1. Jennifer A. Richeson and J. Nicole Shelton, "Negotiating Interracial Interactions: Costs, Consequences, and Possibilities," *Current Directions in Psychological Science* 16, no. 6 (2007): 316–320, https://doi.org/10.1111/j.1467-8721.2007.00528.x.

2. Melanie McFarland, "'Insecure' in the Workplace: Issa Rae Nails the Frustrations of Being Black at the Office." *Salon*, October 28, 2016, https://www.salon.com/2016/10/27/insecure-in-the-workplace-issa-rae-nails-the-frustration-of-being-black-at-the-office/.

3. W. E. B. Du Bois, *The Souls of Black Folk; Essays and Sketches* (New York: Johnson Reprint Corp., 1968).

4. Specifically, the authors find that "relative to white skin, the odds of arrest are 31 percent and 76 percent higher for those with medium brown and black skin, respectively." The authors argue that "that these patterns are suggestive of the existence of structural racism and colorism as well as differential enforcement in the Criminal Justice System." See Jessica G. Finkeldey and Stephen Demuth, "Race/Ethnicity, Perceived Skin Color, and the Likelihood of Adult Arrest," *Race and Justice* 11, no. 4 (2021): 567–591.

5. For more excellent resources and suggestions, see this recent paper: NiCole T. Buchanan, Marisol Perez, Mitchell J. Prinstein, and Idia B. Thurston, "Upending Racism in Psychological Science: Strategies to Change How Science Is Conducted, Reported, Reviewed, and Disseminated," *American Psychologist* 76 (2021): 1097–1112, https://doi.org/10.1037/amp0000905.

6. Government Alliance on Race and Equity, "Tools & Resources," accessed March 25, 2024, https://www.racialequityalliance.org/tools-resources/.

CHAPTER 8

1. In the past, researchers have often used the language of "diagnose" to describe this phase. This framing is problematic because it suggests that the "problem" lies within the individual, not the system. And using the term "diagnose" compares a community's challenge to an illness. Further, a "diagnosis" implies a certainty that may come with medical screenings but rarely is as straightforward when it comes to unpacking the complex web of barriers around behaviors.

2. Asaph Glosser, Dan Cullinan, and Emmi Obara, *Simplify, Notify, Modify: Using Behavioral Insights to Increase Incarcerated Parents' Requests for Child Support Modifications* (Washington, DC: Office of Planning, Research, and Evaluation, 2016).

3. Amelia Gavin, Nancy Grote, Kyaien Conner, and Taurmini Fentress, "Racial Discrimination and Preterm Birth among African American Women: The Important Role of Posttraumatic Stress Disorder," *Journal of Health Disparities Research and Practice* 11, no. 4 (2019), https://digitalscholarship.unlv.edu/jhdrp/vol11/iss4/6.

4. Julie L. Ozanne and Bige Saatcioglu, "Participatory Action Research," *Journal of Consumer Research* 35, no. 3 (2008): 423–439, https://doi.org/10.1086/586911.

5. India has relatively progressive and thoughtful laws to protect sex workers, though they are not always followed as intended.

6. As some PAR researchers have written about, care must be taken to engage partners of color in an equitable fashion when engaging in community research. We include some resources for those who would like to learn more.

7. William F. Funk, "The Paperwork Reduction Act: Paperwork Reduction Meets Administrative Law," *Harvard Journal on Legislation* 24 (1987): 1.

CHAPTER 9

1. Watson is often credited for this quote but has explained that the phrase is not hers alone. It came out of work with an Aboriginal rights group in Queensland in the 1970s.

2. Crystal C. Hall, Jiaying Zhao, and Eldar Shafir, "Self-Affirmation among the Poor: Cognitive and Behavioral Implications," *Psychological Science* 25, no. 2 (2014): 619–625.

3. Office of Evaluation Sciences, "Integrating Health Care Services in Nigeria," accessed March 28, 2024, https://oes.gsa.gov/projects/aligning-healthcare-services-nigeria/.

4. Neil A. Lewis Jr. and J. Frank Yates, "Preparing Disadvantaged Students for Success in College: Lessons Learned from the Preparation Initiative," *Perspectives on Psychological Science* 14, no. 1 (2019): 54–59.

CHAPTER 10

1. In fact, this is why many schools and programs are beginning to either drop or decrease the emphasis on SAT and GRE test scores for admissions decisions.

2. Mary K. Gugerty and Dean Karlan, *The Goldilocks Challenge: Right-Fit Evidence for the Social Sector* (Oxford: Oxford University Press, 2018).

3. Ta-Nehisi Coates, *Between the World and Me* (New York: Spiegel & Grau, 2015).

4. Schuette v. BAMN, 572 US 701, 740 (2014) (Sotomayor, J., dissenting).

5. Jamilia J. Blake et al., "The Role of Colorism in Explaining African American Females' Suspension Risk," *School Psychology Quarterly* 32, no. 1 (2017): 118–130, https://doi.org/10

.1037/spq0000173; Lance Hannon, Robert DeFina, and Sarah Bruch, "The Relationship between Skin Tone and School Suspension for African Americans," *Race and Social Problems* 5, no. 4 (2013): 281–295, https://doi.org/10.1007/s12552-013-9104-z.

6. Some survey instruments ask the interviewer to rate the survey participant's skin tone on a color scale, while others ask the survey participant to self-select their skin tone from a color scale. There is some evidence of "interviewer effects"; specifically, that white and Black interviewers over- and underestimate the darkness of Black and white respondents, respectively, relative to interviewers of the same respondent color. Validation analyses can ensure that interviewer effects on skin color do not bias substantive results. Surveys like the National Longitudinal Survey of Youth collect interviewer IDs and demographic data that can be included in multilevel models that include random effects for interviewers and the interviewer characteristics as control variables.

7. Intersectionality has roots in Black feminist activism, tracing back to Sojourner Truth's 1851 speech at the Women's Rights Convention, where she described her lived experience at the nexus of gender, class, and race inequality. See Nikol G. Alexander-Floyd, "Disappearing Acts: Reclaiming Intersectionality in the Social Sciences in a Post-Black Feminist Era," *Feminist Formations* 24, no. 1 (2012): 1–25.

8. Kimberlé Crenshaw, "Why Intersectionality Can't Wait," *Washington Post*, October 28, 2021, https://www.washingtonpost.com/news/in-theory/wp/2015/09/24/why-intersectionality-cant-wait/.

9. Lisa A. Gennetian et al., "Supplemental Nutrition Assistance Program (SNAP) Benefit Cycles and Student Disciplinary Infractions," *Social Service Review* 90, no. 3 (2016): 403–433.

10. Crystal C. Hall and Ines Jurcevic, *Behavioral Insights for Public Policy: Contextualizing Our Science* (Cambridge, UK: Cambridge University Press, 2022).

11. Jalil B. Mustaffa and Jonathan C. W. Davis, "Jim Crow Debt: How Black Borrowers Experience Student Loans," Education Trust, 2021.

12. National Institutes of Health BRAIN Initiative, "Plan for Enhancing Diverse Perspectives," accessed March 28, 2024, https://braininitiative.nih.gov/vision/plan-enhancing-diverse-perspectives.

CHAPTER 11

1. Benjamin Collins and Cassandria Dortch, "The FAFSA Simplification Act," Congressional Research Service, August 4, 2022, https://crsreports.congress.gov/product/pdf/R/R46909.

2. Brittany Murray, Elsa Falkenburger, and Priya Saxena, "Data Walks: An Innovative Way to Share Data with Communities," June 4, 2016, https://policycommons.net/artifacts/632210/data-walks/1613522/.

3. Andre M. Perry, *Know Your Price: Valuing Black Lives and Property in America's Black Cities* (Washington, DC: Brookings Institution Press, 2020).

4. NiCole T. Buchanan, Marisol Perez, Mitchell J. Prinstein, and Idia B. Thurston, "Upending Racism in Psychological Science: Strategies to Change How Science Is Conducted, Reported, Reviewed, and Disseminated," *The American Psychologist* 76, no. 7 (2021): 1097–1112.

5. Emily Baumgaertner and Farnaz Fassihi, "Racism and Sexism Underlie Higher Maternal Death Rates for Black Women, U.N. Says," *New York Times*, July 12, 2023, https://www.nytimes.com/2023/07/12/health/maternal-deaths-americas-un.html.

6. Katherine D. Hoerster, Evalynn Romano, Barbara I. Baquero, K. L. Shannon, Robert Getch, Rachel Berney, Dori Rosenberg, Stephen Mooney, Brian Saelens, and Crystal Hall, "Process and Early Insights from the PATHSS Study (Participatory Active Transportation for Health in South Seattle): A Model for Community Engagement to Address Climate and Health Impacts," *Annals of Behavioral Medicine* 55 (2021): S535.

7. This is one of several excellent points from the Urban Institute, "Confronting Structural Racism in Research and Policy Analysis: Charting a Course for Policy Research Institutions," which is listed in the resource section.

8. See the blog of the London School of Economics for an example: Alice Chautard, "Inclusive Conferences? We Can and Must Do Better—Here's How," London School of Economics, June 6, 2019, https://blogs.lse.ac.uk/impactofsocialsciences/2019/06/06/inclusive-conferences-we-can-and-must-do-better-heres-how/.

CHAPTER 12

1. National Center for Education Statistics, "Characteristics of Postsecondary Faculty," last updated August 2023, https://nces.ed.gov/programs/coe/indicator/csc; US Census Bureau, "Quick Facts: United States, 2021," last updated July 1, 2023, https://www.census.gov/quickfacts/fact/table/US/PST045221.

2. American Psychological Association. "Minority Fellowship Program (MFP)," accessed March 29, 2024, https://www.apa.org/pi/mfp/.

3. Richard Delgado and Jean Stefancic, *Critical Race Theory, Fourth Edition: An Introduction* (New York: New York University Press, 2023).

4. John A. Powell, "Post-Racialism or Targeted Universalism," *Denver Law Review* 86 (2008): 785.

5. Citations have implications for who gets a voice in academia. Who is being cited can influence promotions, research leadership positions, and speaking engagements. Citation audits can help provide a sense of the ethnic, racial, and gender diversity of your references. However, they aren't perfectly accurate and cannot account for aspects of diversity like gender, sexual identity, and (dis)ability. In addition to citation audits, researchers should expand their universe of research and academic partners.

6. In addition to citation auditing, practices to actively avoid white-centered research practices can include identifying and practicing the use of systems-centered language, calling attention

to majority or exclusively white samples in studies, and crafting thoughtful positionality statements. We have provided some resources to help you get started on this in your own work.

7. Sakaria L. Auelùa-Toomey and Steven O. Roberts, "The Effects of Editorial-Board Diversity on Race Scholars and Their Scholarship: A Field Experiment," *Perspectives on Psychological Science* 17, no. 6 (2022): 1766–1777, https://doi.org/10.1177/17456916211072851.

8. C. Nguyen, "Black Students and Faculty Reflect on 48% Increase in Black Tenured Faculty since 2016," *Daily Bruin*, June 22, 2020, https://dailybruin.com/2020/06/22/black-students-and-faculty-reflect-on-48-increase-in-black-tenured-faculty-since-2016.

9. Not even class!

10. "The Racial Wealth Gap: What Is It and What Can We Do About It?" Ford Foundation, https://www.fordfoundation.org/ideas/equals-change-blog/posts/the-racial-wealth-gap-what-is-it-and-what-can-we-do-about-it/.

11. The NIH tells researchers that their PEDP should include items that advance inclusivity in research. These items might include a description of plans to enhance recruiting of women and individuals from groups traditionally underrepresented in the biomedical, behavioral, and clinical research workforce; monitoring activities to identify and measure PEDP progress benchmarks; and planned engagement activities to enhance recruitment of individuals from diverse groups as research participants, including those from underrepresented backgrounds.

12. Steven Brown, Graham MacDonald, and Claire Bowen, "How the Federal Government Can Use Data to Make the Most of the Executive Order on Racial Equity," Urban Institute, January 29, 2021, https://www.urban.org/urban-wire/how-federal-government-can-use-data-make-most-executive-order-racial-equity.

CHAPTER 13

1. Eric Angner, "Epistemic Humility and Coronavirus: Knowing Your Limits in a Pandemic," *Behavioral Scientist*, February 26, 2020, https://behavioralscientist.org/epistemic-humility-coronavirus-knowing-your-limits-in-a-pandemic/.

2. For more on the history of this period and the national anthem, see this Pulitzer Prize-winning book: Alan Taylor, *The Internal Enemy: Slavery and War in Virginia, 1772–1832* (New York: WW Norton & Company, 2013).

3. Library of Congress, "US Poet Laureate Ada Limón Opening Reading," September 29, 2022, https://www.loc.gov/item/webcast-10554.

Index

Note: Page numbers in italics indicate references to figures.

Academic collaborations, 87
Academic journals, 46, 49, 80, 123, 128
Academics, action agenda for, 125–128
"Achievement gap," 163n7
Actionability, 108
Action agenda, 125–133
Administrative data, creative use of, 113
"Advancing Racial Equity and Support for Underserved Communities through the Federal Government" (Executive Order 13985), 11–12
Advertising, 10–11, 42–43, 44
Air pollution, x
Algorithmic discrimination, 13–14
Allcott, Hunt, 34
American National Election Studies, 110
American Psychological Association (APA), 13, 49, 129
American Psychological Foundation, 126
American Sociological Association conference, 50
AmericasBarometer study, 110
Angner, Eric, 136
Antiracist practices
    checklists for, 83–84, 90, 95–96, 103, 115–116, 124
    definition of, 79

Applied behavioral science
    avoidance of structural racism and, 4–5, 38–39
    biases and, 22–25, 37–38
    defining antiracist approach to, 70–74
    examples of, 33–35
    focus on individual and, 10, 24–27
    global interest in, 1–2
    key insights and critical oversights of, 19–32
    as new field, 135–136
    potential of, 136
    underreliance on social psychology and, 27–31
Aronson, Elliot, 53–54
Aronson, Joshua, 31
"Arrested mobility," 44, 82
Artificial intelligence (AI), 13–14
Auelua-Toomey, Sakaria L., 128
Authorship, 67–68, 88
"Awarding gap," 163n7

Bank on DC, 69–70
Batson, Daniel, 28–29
Behavioral intervention design
    traditional approach to, 55–56
    updated model for, 57–68, *58*, *62*, *64*
Behavioral maps, 43–44, 55–56, 61, *62*, *64*

Behavioral science, antiracist application of, 8
Behavioral Scientist, ix, 136
Behavioural Insights Team (BIT), 26, 34
Belonging, importance of, 9
Benartzi, Schlomo, 33
BIAS (Behavioral Interventions to Advance Self-Sufficiency) project, 38, 91, 95
Biases, 19–20, 22–25, 29, 37–38, 100–101, 121–122
Biden, Joe, 11–12, 14
Biking example, 43–44, 63, 71–72, 82, 106–107, 114
Biomedical research, 81
BIPOC partners, recruiting and supporting, 80–81
Black Lives Matter protests, 5
Blige, Mary J., 3
Boomerang effect, 160n5
Boston Globe, The, 79
Bounded rationality, 21
Bronx Science, 85–86
Brown, Charles, 44, 82
Brown v. Board of Education, 52, 53, 112
Buchanan, NiCole T., 122
Budgeting, 115, 130
Burey, Jodi-Ann, 85
Bystander intervention, 28–29

Calcification, 13
Cameron, David, 1–2
Canned laughter, 25
Chater, Nick, 10, 26
ChatGPT, 14
Childcare, event attendance and, 124
Child support modifications, 91–92
Cialdini, Robert, 158n18
Citation audits, 127
Civil Rights Movement, 13
Clark, Kenneth and Mamie, 52–53, 70, 112
Climate crisis, x, 26
Coates, Ta-Nehisi, 33, 108
CoDesign, *58*, 65–66, 97–103

CoDiscover, *58*, 60–65, 91–96
College debt, 39–41, 60, 72–73, 102, 114
Colonialism, 154n4
Colorblind, meaning of, 6
Colorism, 89, 109–110, 111, 131
Color silent, 5
Community-Based Participatory Research Program, 57
Complexity avoidance, 22–23, 39
Conferences, action agenda involving, 128
Consumer research, 25–26
Correspondence bias, 29
COVID-19 pandemic, x, 4, 5
Crear-Perry, Joia, 7
Credibility, 107
Crenshaw, Kimberlé, 111, 155n12
Critical race theory, 127, 129
Cultural literacy, 77

Daily Show, The, 79
Darity, William, Jr., 37, 79–80
Darley, John, 28–29
Data sharing, 132
Data Walk, 119–120
Davis, Angela, 1, 78
Davis, Jonathan, 114
Debt, college. *See* College debt
Debt-to-assets ratio, 37
DellaVigna, Stefano, 160n10
Desegregation, 53–54
"Diagnose," use of term, 166n1
DiAngelo, Robin, 48
Differential impacts, 118
Disaggregation, nuanced, 109–111
Dissemination events, 123–124
Diversity
  authentic partnerships and, 86–88
  dissemination events and, 123–124
  editorial boards and, 128
  faculty and, 129
  in feedback sources, 67
  inclusive evaluations and, 108–109
  lack of, 25, 31–32, 45–46

Diversity and Inclusion Committee for the Society of Judgment and Decision Making, 128
Doll study, 52–53, 70, 112–113
Domestic violence, 78
Double consciousness, 87–88
Douglass, Frederick, 125
Doulas, 8–9, 103
Du Bois, W. E. B., 87–88
Du Bois Review, 50

Earned Income Tax Credit (EITC), 14, 35–36
Ease, maximizing, 22
EAST framework, 158n10
Ebony, 162n35
Editorial boards, 128
Education. *See also* College debt
 disparities in, 78
 financial aid and, 39–41
 financial returns on, 3
 opportunity gap and, 48
 planning intervention regarding, 85–86
 of self and team, 83–84
Education savings accounts, 35
Employment discrimination, 20, 41, 61.
 See also Hiring decisions/systems
Energy efficient behaviors, 33–34
Epistemic humility, 136
Equity action plans, 12
Evaluation, designing, 65–66, 105–116
Evidence of behavior, 24–25
Executive Order 13707, "Using Behavioral Science Insights to Better Serve the American People," 34
Executive Order 13985, "Advancing Racial Equity and Support for Underserved Communities through the Federal Government," 11–12
Executive Order 14091, "Furthering Advancing Racial Equity and Support for Underserved Communities through the Federal Government," 11–12

FAFSA. *See* US Free Application for Federal Student Aid (FAFSA)
Fans, action agenda for, 132–133
Federal Reserve Bank, 79
Floyd, George, ix, xi, 5, 121
Food and Drug Administration (FDA), 10–11
Ford Foundation, 130
Formative research, 93–94
Framing, 27
Free and reduced-price lunch (FRPL) program, 105–106, 107, 109, 113
Fundamental attribution error, 29
Funders, action agenda for, 129–131
Funding, lack of, 48–50
"Furthering Advancing Racial Equity and Support for Underserved Communities through the Federal Government" (Executive Order 14091), 11–12

Galbraith, John Kenneth, 107
Galeano, Eduardo, 77
Gatekeepers, 127
Gemini (Google AI), 14
General Social Survey, 110
Gennetian, Lisa, 113
Goals
 intentional, 78–80
 present bias and, 23–24
Goldilocks Challenge, The (Gugerty and Karlan), 107–108
Good Place, The, 21–22
Good Samaritan experiment, 28–29
Gorman, Amanda, 136
Government Alliance on Race and Equity's (GARE) Racial Equity Toolkit, 90
Graduate Record Examination (GRE), 31
Graduation rates, 40, 41
Grant, Adam, 30
Grit, 30
Group cohesion, 53
Group conflict theory, 53
Group norms, 53
Gugerty, Mary K., 107–108

Hallsworth, Michael, 26
Hamilton, Darrick, 37, 79–80, 146
Health care
    access to, 3–4, 7–9
    costs of, 37
Health insurance, 37
Heuristics (shortcuts), 19–21
Hiring decisions/systems, 20, 126–127, 132
hooks, bell, 80
Housing insecurity, 39
How to Be an Antiracist (Kendi), 9

ideas42, 35, 57, 166n1
Ideation design process, 56
IDEO, 56
Immigration status, 114–115
    Implement and Interpret, 58, 66–67, 105–116
Incarceration, 78, 91–92
Incentive structures, 48–50
Inclusive design, 56, 98–100, 115, 131
Inclusivity, 108
Income inequality, 2. *See also* Wealth gap
Individual, focus on, 10, 25–27
Infant mortality, 4, 7, 122
Informational interviews, 99
In-person design workshops, 99
Insecure, 87–88
Institutional Review Board, 115
Internal Revenue Service (IRS), 14
Interracial partnerships, difficulty of, 87–88
Intersectional approach, 111–112, 120, 155n12
Intersectionality, 78, 111, 155n12
Interventions, designing, 56, 65–66
Interviewer effects, 168n6
Invisible labor, 87

Jay-Z, 3
"Jigsaw classroom," 53–54, 103
Job readiness programs, 38
Journal editors, 46, 49, 80, 125

Journal of Economic Inequality, 50
Journal of Economics, Race, and Policy, 50
Journal of Race and Class, 49
Jumpstart, 98
Jurcevic, Ines, 114

Kahneman, Daniel, 2, 21
Karlan, Dean, 107–108
Kendi, Ibram X., 5, 7, 8, 9, 70
Keywords, inclusive, 123
King, Martin Luther, Jr., 13, 156n22
Kozhimannil, Katy, 9

Language, formal versus informal, 159n24
Laskey, Alex, 33–34
Latin American Public Opinion Project, 110
Lewis, Neil, 101
Limitations, acknowledging, 82–83
Limón, Ada, ix, 135, 137
Linos, Elizabeth, 159n24, 160n10
Lived experience
    authentic partnerships and, 86–87
    centering, 123
    hiring decisions and, 132
    importance of, 60
    lack of attention to, 77, 91–92
Loans, denial of, 2
Loewenstein, George, 10, 26
London School of Economics, 124
Lorde, Audre, 91
Los Angeles Unified School District (LAUSD), 105–106, 107, 109, 113
Loss aversion, 33

Machine learning, 13–14
Mass incarceration, 78
Maternal health, 7–9
Maternal mortality, 4, 103, 122
Maximizing utility, 19, 22
MDRC, 161n18
Medicaid, 7, 9
Medicare Part D, 22

Medication adherence, 95
Mental bandwidth, 21
Menthol cigarettes, 11, 42–43, 100–101
Messengers, 43
Minority Fellowship Program (MFP) Fund for Racial and Ethnic Diversity, 126
Mobility challenges, 122–123
Mozart, Wolfgang Amadeus, 30
Muñoz, Ana Patricia, 79–80
Mustaffa, Jalil B., 114

National Bureau of Economics Research, 50
National Conference on Race and Ethnicity in Higher Education, 50
National Longitudinal Survey of Youth, 110
National Science Foundation (NSF), 49, 129–130
Neoclassical economic theory, 19–21
Neutrality, absence of, 70
"New National Anthem" (Limón), ix, 135, 137
News outlets, sharing results with, 122–123
New York Times, The, 122
Nisbett, Richard, 50–51
Noah, Trevor, 77
Nonexperimental evaluations, 65–66
Nontraditional metrics, 113
"Non-white" populations, grouping, 118
Nudge, 25
Nudge Unit (UK), 34
Nudging, 6, 10

Obama, Barack, 1–2, 38, 156n22
Office, The, 80
Office of Data Equity, 132
Office of Evaluation Sciences (OES), 39, 75
Office of Extramural Research, 81
Office of Management and Budget, 132
Oluo, Ijeoma, 82, 105
Open science movement, 127
Opower, 33–34
Opportunity gap in schools, 48

Oracle, 34
Organisation for Economic Co-operation and Development (OECD), 34

Paperwork Reduction Act (PRA), 94–95, 131
Parker, Theodore, 156n22
Participatory action research (PAR), 94
Participatory process, 119–120
Participatory research methods, 129
Partner and CoDefine, 58, 59–60, 85–90
Partnerships
    design stage and, 98
    forging authentic, 86–88
    fundraising and, 88
    interracial, 87–88
    results and, 122–123
Pasquale, Frank, 10
Pension Protection Act (2006), 33
Perry, Andre, 121
Person and the Situation, The (Ross and Nisbett), 50–51
Pew Research Center, 83
Pilot testing, 99–100
"Plan for Enhancing Diverse Perspectives (PEDP)," 115, 131
Police violence
    fear of, 44, 63, 72, 82
    gaps in understanding of, 78
Policymakers, action agenda for, 131–132
Practitioners, action agenda for, 131–132
Pregnancy complications, 4, 92–93, 103, 122
Prejudice reduction strategies, 83
Prepaid cards, 69–70
Preparation Initiative, 101
Prescription drug example, 22–23
Present bias, 22, 23, 33
Preterm births, 92–93
Privilege, acknowledging, 82–83
Proactive antiracism, 78
Profiling, 44, 63, 72, 82, 114
Promotion systems, 126–127

Prosperity Now, 36
Psychological taxes, 114

Qualitative methods
   expanding training in, 127, 129
   leveraging, 112–113
Quasi-experimental evaluations, 66

Race-based hiring discrimination, 20. *See also* Employment discrimination; Hiring decisions/systems
Race-conscious frameworks, 127, 129
Race neutral, meaning of, 6
Race theory, 77
Racial concordance, 9
Racial equity tools, 90
Racial stamina, lack of, 48
Racism. *See also* Structural racism
   acknowledging structural, 103, 121–122
   discomfort with, 47–48
   gaps in understanding of, 77–78
   outdated definition of, 47
Rae, Issa, 87–88
Randomized controlled trials (RCTs), 66, 105–107
Rankine, Claudia, 45
Rational actor theory, 19–21, 22, 33
Reagan, Natalia, 135
Recommendations, using participatory process and, 119–120
Redlining, 20, 44, 61, 78, 82
Representation, 80–81
Research
   formative, 93–94
   participatory, 129
   participatory action, 94
Responsibilization, 25–26
Results
   nuance and, 120
   using participatory process and, 119–120
ReThinking (podcast), 30
Retirement accounts, 2, 19–20, 33, 35, 37

Review of Black Political Economy, 50
"RFA-MH-21-180" (NIH funding mechanism), 131
Richeson, Jennifer, 87, 88
"Right-fit" evaluation, 107–108
Rizzo, Michael, 78
Robbers Cave experiment, 53–54
Roberts, Steven O., 78, 80, 128
Rock, Chris, 3
Rogers, Todd, 34
Ross, Lee, 50–51
Roy, Arundhati, 69

Save More Tomorrow intervention, 33, 34
Savings, 51–52. *See also* Retirement accounts
Savings bonds, 35
School of Machine and Metal Trade (New York), 86
Segregation
   Brown v. Board of Education and, 52, 53, 112
   history of, 71
   impact of, 52
Sex workers' rights, 94
Share, Adapt, Scale, 58, 67–68, 117–124
Shelton, Nicole, 87, 88
Sherif, Muzafer, 53
SIMPLER, 158n10
Simplification, 23, 73, 102, 119, 159n24
Situational factors, impact of, 6
Situationism, 28–30
Slavery, 77
Small-scale pilot testing, 99–100
Smoking, 10–11, 41–43, 44, 100–101
Social and Behavioral Sciences Team (SBST), 2, 38–39, 40, 99, 131
Social comparison, 24
Social influence, 22, 24–25
Social proof, 24, 42
Social psychology
   leveraging insights from, 114
   underreliance on, 25, 27–31
Social referents, 42

Society for Personality and Social Psychology, 127
Society for the Psychological Study of Culture, Ethnicity, and Race Research conference, 50
Society for Judgment and Decision Making, 128
Sociology of Race and Ethnic Relations Conference, 50
Sotomayor, Sonia, 108
Southern Poverty Law Center, 77
Southwest Center for Human Relations Studies, 50
Spriggs, William, 121
Staff, recruiting and supporting BIPOC, 80–81, 126
Standardized test scores, 107
Stanovich, Keith, 158n9
Steele, Claude, 30–31
Stereotype threat, 28, 31
Stratification economics, 157n6
Structural biases, 100–101, 121–122
Structural racism
  acknowledging, 103, 121
  in biomedical research, 81
  fight against, 130
  focus on, 132
  lack of attention to, 4, 25, 38–39, 49, 50
  meaning of, 4
  wealth gap and, 2
Student loans, 60. *See also* College debt
Students
  action agenda for, 128–129
  recruiting and supporting BIPOC, 126
Subgroups, reporting results and, 120
Summer Youth Employment Program (SYEP), 69–70
Supplemental Nutrition Assistance Program (SNAP), 113
System 1 versus System 2 mental processes, 21–22
Systemic detractors, 63, 89–90

Systemic racism, executive orders and, 11–12
Systems-based approach, 63
Systems-centered language, 122, 130, 169n6
Systems-level analysis, 77, 89–90

Targeted universalism, 127, 129
Tatum, Beverly Daniel, 55, 155n9
Tax returns/tax preparation center, 1, 2–3, 14, 35–36, 51
Teach for America, 163n7
Temporary Assistance for Needy Families (TANF), 38
Thaler, Richard, 33
Thinking, Fast and Slow (Kahneman), 21
Time-inconsistent preferences, 23
Tobacco industry, 41–43
Tobacco use, 10–11, 41–43, 44, 100–101
Training, 83
Truth, Sojourner, 168n7
Tversky, Amos, 2

Unbanked households, 69–70
Underrepresentation in research teams, 31–32
Unintended consequences, anticipating and designing for, 101–102, 113–115
UK Behavioural Insights Team (BIT), 2
University of California Los Angeles (UCLA) Black Graduate Student Association, 129
Urban Institute, 119–120, 124, 132
US Agency for International Development, 99
US Bureau of Labor Statistics, 131
US Census Bureau, x, 132
US Civil War, 77
US Department of Education, 39
US Department of Health and Human Services, 35, 37–38
US FAFSA Simplification Act (2020), 119
US Free Application for Federal Student Aid (FAFSA), 23, 39–41, 65, 71, 72–74, 102, 114, 119

US National Institutes of Health (NIH), 46, 57, 81, 115, 131
US National Institutes of Health Brain Research through Advancing Innovative Neurotechnologies (BRAIN) initiative, 115, 131
US Treasury Department, 14

Value-creating system-level change, 10
Volunteer Income Tax Assistance (VITA) sites, 35–36, 51. *See also* Tax returns/tax preparation center
Voter ID laws, 6
Voting initiatives, 119
Voting rights, 6

Wage gaps, 2
Waheed, Nayyirah, 5–6
Walker, Alice, 117
Walker, Darren, 130
Washington, Denzel, 3
Watson, Lilla, 97
Wealth gap, 3, 26, 65, 74, 79, 121, 130
WEIRD (Western, Educated, Industrialized, Rich, and Democratic) populations, 31–32
West, Richard, 158n9
White-centered research practices, disruption of, 127
White fragility, 48
White House Office of Science and Technology Policy (OSTP), 38
Wilkerson, Isabel, 19
Women's Rights Convention, 168n7
World Resources Institute, 82
Wood, Roy, Jr., 79
Workplace, preparing, 77–84

Yates, Dan, 33–34
Yates, Frank, 101